COFFEE
coffee
COFFEE
AF516649

URBAN DESI

Non-Vegetarian

VICKY RATNANI

Om Books International

First published in 2022 by

Corporate & Editorial Office
A-12, Sector 64, Noida 201 301
Uttar Pradesh, India
Phone: +91 120 477 4100
Email: editorial@ombooks.com
Website: www.ombooksinternational.com

Sales Office
107, Ansari Road, Darya Ganj, New Delhi 110 002, India
Phone: +91 11 4000 9000
Email: sales@ombooks.com
Website: www.ombooks.com

Editors: Ipshita Mitra, Anukriti Singh, Simran Kaur

Photographers: Aashish Chauhan, Vinayak Grover, Piyush Singh Charag

ISBN: 9789352766338

Printed in India

10 9 8 7 6 5 4 3 2 1

To
all who
eat to
live

Is your pet in pain?
Cheating your way through parties
What is so English about hope?

Contents

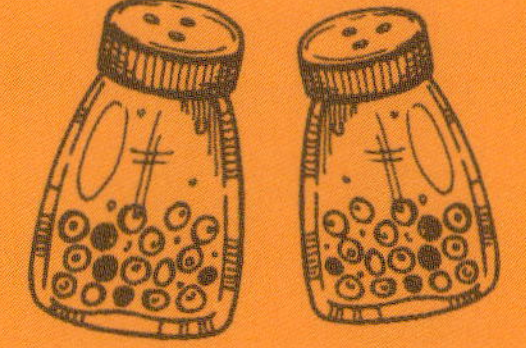

FOREWORD

Fasten your seat belts because this is not a mere cookbook, it's Vicky's taste-travel through India and even through time. Pouring over it, each recipe gave me as much pleasure as dining at his award-winning restaurants and watching his TV shows. His memorable oomph of flavour and reverence for seasonal ingredients has always shone whether it was as the Executive Chef at the office of Queen Elizabeth II or his action in Peru and Australia while shooting his YouTube videos.

What knits all Vicky's work together is high-octane creativity rooted in tradition, a thrilling sense of adventure and the ability to share this, whether it is through food or films or books. Through his book *Urban Desi* this multi-talented chef whizzes us on a culinary journey that is saturated in the rich culture and heritage across the Indian subcontinent. Vicky goes back into time and handpicks the rare Gosht Ka Halwa from Rampur, Keema from Rajasthan, unusual Gondhuraj Lemon Chicken from Bengal and more. Street food finds equal pride of place, be it the Bhujing from streets of Virar in Mumbai or Dimer Devil from Bengal. Even his family's precious legacy of recipes, be it his mother's Sindhi Mutton or the Brain Pakoda from his sister-in-law's kitchen is shared with us through this book. He has included crowd-pleaser street food with equal panache as he does rare royal recipes.

Presented as an exotic spread, each of these recipes is meticulously crafted with invaluable introduction and handy tips. While Vicky serves up the best of the Indian subcontinent, he takes care to ensure that you don't have to look for ingredients further that your regular Indian grocery store. Useful and usable, each recipe is tried, tasted and tested, this cookbook is your go-to guide to whip up a delicious meal. So go ahead, sink your teeth into it and relish the taste of India.

Note: Here's some good news for you – as we are enjoying Urban Desi (non-veg), Vicky is cooking up Urban Desi (veg).

RASHMI UDAY SINGH
Award-winning author of
40 cookbooks, food critic
and TV host

Introduction

There is something elementally appealing about food, don't you think? Some of us eat to live while the rest of us live to eat and I am a proud member of team – live to eat. So if you are holding this book, I would like to believe that we are on the same team.

My fascination with food began as a child. It went from being curious about food to being awed as I watched people relish the food I cooked for them. If you ask me what fascinates me about food, I would say – everything. It transcends social and personal boundaries, forms the cornerstone of the cultures around the world and more importantly, it evokes strong feelings in people.

Speaking of strong feelings, I found a home away from home in food. I am sure all of us, whether far from home or not have a specific dish or a cuisine that we carry with us in our heart. When I decided to write this book, I thought to myself why not start from the country I was born in?

Contrary to popular belief, Indian food is a lot more than just naan and curries; cuisines of the Indian diaspora are as diverse as one can imagine. The country is flanked by the Himalayas in the north, the arid deserts on the west, while the peninsula is ensconced in the Indian Ocean. This gives India a varied topography – from snow capped peaks and sweltering beaches to the deserts hosting a myriad of communities foraging for food and making it their own. The history of these cuisines is as beautiful as the people who have lived it and made it.

Having scaled the length and breadth of India, my biggest learning from it is that there is always scope for innovation when it comes to Indian food. I have kept this lesson in mind while curating these recipes. *Urban Desi* is an amalgam of what you find in the city streets and what you get once you go off the beaten track. Each recipe has been put together to bring out the best of the Indian subcontinent, without having you to look for ingredients further than your regular Indian grocery store. It sates your palate yet it doesn't have you toiling over the stove.

Go ahead, embark on a culinary journey rooted in the rich culture and heritage of India with some of the handpicked recipes. This is not a coffee table book, so if you find yourself with a copy, I expect it to have a couple of stains and perhaps slightly doggy eared. Explore India through food, one dish at a time with this book albeit Vicky style!

SURF

salt.

Cullieo Crab Cakes

30 minutes | Serves 4-6

IN A NUTSHELL

Subtly spiced Goan style crab cakes are made with basic spices and condiments. Savour this with a salad and dip of your choice. Ideal for dinner parties or a potluck meal, you can use different portion sizes to make cakes, patty, appetisers, and more!

INGREDIENTS

½ kg potatoes, boiled and skinned

½ kg crabmeat

1 tsp turmeric

4 small green chillies, deseeded and finely chopped

3 tsps red chilli powder

1 tsp black pepper

2 tsps lime juice

Salt to taste

Oil to fry

3 eggs, beaten

7 tbsps breadcrumbs

METHOD

- Mash potatoes in a large mixing bowl.
- Add crabmeat and mash again to mix them well.
- Add turmeric, green chillies, red chilli powder, black pepper, lime juice, and salt.
- Season with salt. Mix well.
- Divide into 1 inch or similar sized balls, flatten and cover with a moist cloth.
- Heat oil in a frying pan.
- In a shallow bowl, place the beaten eggs and in another put breadcrumbs.
- Coat both sides of the cutlet first with eggs and breadcrumbs and slide it into the fryer.
- Serve hot with a condiment of your choice.

Green Spice Lobster

 30 minutes | Serves 

IN A NUTSHELL

Delectable lobster tails ensconced in robust green spices sounds appetizing, doesn't it? This high on spice marinade adds the volume to the luxurious lobster meat, making it a simple yet impressive main course!

INGREDIENTS

2 lobster tails, 600 gms each
1 ½ cups cilantro leaves
1 ½ cups mint leaves
4 green chillies
½ tsp black pepper powder
½ tsp red chilli powder
1 tsp garam masala
½ tsp dry mango powder
1 tsp cumin powder
1 tsp coriander powder
2 tbsps ginger-garlic paste
½ cup hung yoghurt
2 lobster tails-600 gms each
4 tbsps ghee (clarified butter)
Lemon wedges to garnish
Chaat masala to garnish

METHOD

- In a blender, combine washed cilantro leaves, mint leaves and green chillies and grind into a fine paste. Add a tsp of water if required.
- Add the rest of the spices (i.e. black pepper, red chilli, garam masala, dry mango, cumin and coriander powder along with the ginger-garlic paste) to the green paste and mix with the hung yoghurt.
- Marinade the lobster tails with this mixture for an hour.
- Preheat the oven to 190°C.
- Drizzle the tails with clarified butter and bake for 15 minutes.
- Garnish with lemon wedges and chaat masala, and serve with a crisp salad of your choice.

Gudok

(North East Indian Curry)

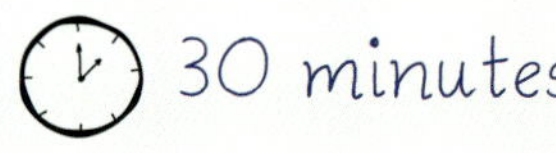

IN A NUTSHELL

Arguably, this dish which is native to the Mog, Tripuri and the Reang tribes of Tripura, holds cultural importance. Gudok is a coarse and mildly flavoured curry made with fermented fish. The recipe in this book is a fairly standard one but many times locals like to add the products available to them such as dried jackfruit seeds, bamboo shoots et al.

INGREDIENTS

2 medium-sized fermented fish, dry roasted

1 cup snake beans (or French beans)

1 medium-sized potato, washed and peeled

Water for boiling the vegetables

Salt for seasoning

2 garlic cloves, peeled

4 green chillies

1 small onion, julienned

Coriander leaves to garnish

METHOD

- Wash the beans and cut them into 1 inch pieces.
- Cube the potatoes and set aside.
- Add beans and potatoes to a pot. Then add just enough water to cover the contents.
- Sprinkle some salt and bring to a boil.
- Add garlic, green chillies and fermented fish. Cover and simmer for 10 minutes.
- Remove from heat and blend the stock and the vegetables together into a coarse thick paste.
- Garnish with julienned onions and coriander.
- Serve hot with rice.

Iromba

30 minutes | Serves 2-3

IN A NUTSHELL

Arguably one of the popular Manipuri dishes in the country, Iromba is a comforting porridge made with potatoes, and smoked and fermented fish that lends it a distinctive smoky flavour. It is lovingly known as the lifeline of the locals. Relished both by vegetarians and non-vegetarians, in the vegetarian variant, fish is replaced with veggies such as yam, beans, et al.

INGREDIENTS

1 cup bamboo shoot, fermented

½ cup smoked fish, flaked

1 cup fermented fish, flaked

1 tbsp canola oil

1 large onion, finely chopped

2 medium-sized potatoes

1 big king chilli

1 cup of vegetables of your choice, boiled

Salt to taste

(fermented and smoked fish can be bought at any shop stocking food products from North-Eastern India)

METHOD

- Boil the fermented bamboo shoot and drain. Set aside.
- In a saucepan, heat oil and add onion, smoked fish, mashed potatoes and king chilli. Mix well.
- Add the fermented fish to the saucepan.
- Add the vegetables to the saucepan and mash them well.
- Add fermented bamboo shoots and mash well. Add salt.
- Stir until it turns into a thick porridge.

Mackerel Pollichathu

Serves 2 (as a main course)

A revered delicacy along the Malabar Coast, Pollichathu is a process of cooking this delicate yet bony fish wrapped in a spice mix in a banana leaf parcel. You can also substitute this fish with pomfret or mackerel like I have in this recipe. Relished as a side or by itself, this fiery sumptuous dish may have one reaching for a glass of water.

INGREDIENTS

1 large mackerel cleaned, about 1kg
1 tbsp coconut oil
A sprig of curry leaves
2 medium-sized onions, julienned
1 medium-sized tomato, chopped
2 green chillies, slit and deseeded
1 inch ginger, grated
4-6 cloves garlic, finely sliced
1½ tsps Kashmiri chilli powder
½ tsp pepper powder
¼ tsp turmeric powder
Salt to taste
1 tsp vinegar
1 banana leaf

FOR MARINATION:

½ Kashmiri chilli powder
¼ tsp turmeric, powdered
1 pinch pepper powder
½ tsp lime juice
½ tsp salt
1 tsp coconut oil

METHOD

- Clean the fish and make three parallel slits on each side.
- Rub in all the marination ingredients. Set aside for 20 minutes.
- Heat a pan and add ½ tsp of coconut oil. Sear both sides of the fish for 30-45 seconds.
- Take the fish off the heat and set aside.
- Heat 1 tbsp coconut oil in the pan and splutter curry leaves.
- Add onion, sauté until transparent. Add tomato, slit green chilli, ginger and garlic. Sauté for three minutes.
- Add chilli, pepper and turmeric powder. Mix well. Season with salt.
- Add vinegar and cook together until the ingredients mix well and turn off the heat.
- Lightly coat both the sides of the banana leaf with oil.
- Heat the pan and sear the leaf on both sides for 5-7 seconds.

- Take off from the heat and slice into two equal parts.
- Place half of the sautéed masala on the leaf, place fish on top of it, and top it off with the rest of the masala and a sprig of curry leaves.
- Fold it in from all four sides and tie it in a parcel.
- Heat the same pan, drizzle some oil and place the parcel in there. Let it cook for 5-7 minutes on both sides. Drizzle a little more oil if you deem fit.
- Untie the string, open the parcel and serve hot.

Muji Gaad

(Kashmiri Radish and Fish Curry)

20 minutes | Serves

A native from the northern most state in the country – Jammu & Kashmir, Muji Gaad is a fish curry unlike any other in the subcontinent. It features the use of radish in the curry, which gives it a peculiar, delicious flavour. Pungent on the aromas and subtle on the spices, the curry seamlessly brings them both together.

4 fillets of rohu, 180 gms each (you could substitute this with tilapia or any other fresh water fish)

½ tsp turmeric powder

½ tsp red chilli powder

Salt to taste

2 tbsps mustard oil

1 medium-sized radish, chopped into large pieces

1 tsp cumin seeds

4 whole cloves

2 pods of green cardamom

1 tbsp Kashmiri red chilli powder

1 tsp fennel powder

½ tsp ginger powder

1 tsp garam masala powder

½ tsp asafoetida

2 green chillies, slit

2 cups water

1 tsp tamarind paste

METHOD

- In a large bowl, marinate the fish with turmeric powder, red chilli powder and salt. Set aside for about an hour.
- Heat oil in a saucepan. Fry radish lightly, transfer into a plate and dab with a paper towel.
- Lightly fry the fish fillet, transfer to another plate, and dab with paper towel.
- In the same saucepan, splutter cumin, cloves and cardamom.
- After this, add Kashmiri red chilli powder, fennel and ginger powder, garam masala, asafoetida and green chillies. Sauté until the ingredients mix well.
- Add 2 cups of water and bring to boil.
- Lower the heat and drop the radish in the gravy and simmer until the gravy thickens.
- When the gravy is close to the desired consistency, add the tamarind paste, fish and water (if needed) and simmer further until the gravy thickens.
- Serve hot with rice.

THE
POT-SHOT!!

THE
POT-SHOT!!

Kerala Dried Fish Chutney

20 minutes | Serves 2-3

INGREDIENTS

1 cup dried anchovy/shrimp

1 tbsp cooking oil

1 small onion, finely chopped

1 cup grated coconut

3 small green chillies, slit

5 tsps lemon juice

IN A NUTSHELL

Arguably Mumbai's oldest original street food, Bhujing is a feisty snack. Conceived on the periphery of the city, Agashi Bhujing Centre in Virar is believed to be the first place to serve it. A popular breakfast favourite of the locals it isn't unsurprising to see this tiny eatery teeming with both locals and the people summoned from far away.

METHOD

- In a small skillet, lightly toast the dried fish. Set aside.
- In the same skillet, add oil and let the onion caramelise.
- In a grinder, add onion, coconut, chillies and lemon juice.
- Grind into a coarse paste.
- Serve a spoonful alongside roti or rice.

Meen Cutlets

(Kerala Style Fish Cutlets)

 50 minutes | Serves 

IN A NUTSHELL

Similar to croquettes, these delicious fish cutlets make for an ideal snack. Make it into an appetiser by rolling into smaller portions or a patty by making a large one and sandwiching it between buns.

INGREDIENTS

250 gms of skinned and deboned fish fillets (preferably Indian salmon or pomfret)

2 tbsps oil

1 large onion, diced

3 green chillies, finely chopped

2 tbsps ginger, minced

4 cloves of garlic, minced

5-8 curry leaves, finely chopped

1 tsp red chilli powder

¼ tsp turmeric powder

½ tsp coriander powder

½ tsp black pepper, powdered

¼ tsp fennel powder

1 tbsp East Indian bottle masala (or any other fish masala)

½ tsp garam masala

2 medium-sized potatoes, boiled

1 egg

½ cup breadcrumbs

Oil to fry

Salt to taste

METHOD

- Heat 2 tbsps oil in a pan. Sauté onions until translucent.
- Add green chillies, ginger, garlic and curry leaves. Sauté for a few more minutes.
- Add red chilli, turmeric, coriander, black pepper and fennel powder. Follow this with the fish masala and garam masala powder. Sauté for two minutes.
- Add the fish fillets to the pan and mix well. Follow the fish with potato mash.
- Mix well and sauté for 10 more minutes. Take off heat and allow the fish and potato mash to cool.
- Do a taste test and add salt if required.
- Make ping-pong sized balls from the fish and potato mix and keep aside.
- In a bowl, beat the egg. In another bowl place the breadcrumbs.
- Heat oil in the fryer.
- Flatten the cutlet balls and give them an egg wash.
- Follow this by coating them with breadcrumbs.
- Fry until golden brown and dab with a paper towel.
- Serve hot with onion salad, chutney or ketchup.

MH 7 MM 137

Kolmi Nu Patio

(Zoroastrian Style Prawn Curry)

40 minutes | Serves 

IN A NUTSHELL

A sweet and sour prawn curry, Kolmi Nu Patio belongs to the affable Parsi community spread across the Indian subcontinent. Usually eaten with brown rice, this prawn (or shrimp) dish is the main course eaten as a part of the traditional Lagan Nu Bhonu. This quick curry is delectable with rice or just usual bread.

INGREDIENTS

- 40 medium-sized prawns, cleaned, deveined, tail and head off
- 1 tbsp oil
- A sprig of curry leaves
- 2 medium-sized onions, finely chopped
- 1 tsp turmeric powder
- 3 tsps cumin powder
- 1 tsp red chilli powder
- 3 cloves garlic, fine chopped (or 2 tsp garlic paste)
- 4 medium-sized tomatoes, blanched and pureed
- 2 tsps sugar
- 1 tbsp vinegar
- Salt to taste
- Water as needed

METHOD

- Heat oil in a saucepan on medium heat and splutter curry leaves.
- Add finely chopped onions and fry until transparent. Sauté further until they start to caramelise.
- Add turmeric and cumin powder and sauté for about a minute. Follow this by red chilli powder.
- Then add garlic and sauté further for another 2 minutes.
- Once the garlic is cooked, add tomato puree and cook for 6-8 minutes on medium heat.
- At this point, if the gravy turns a little thick and vulnerable to the heat (read: may burn), add a tbsp of water and cook further on medium low heat.
- Add prawns, stir to mix well and add a little water.
- In a bowl, mix sugar and vinegar and stir.
- Add this to the pan once the prawns are cooked. Simmer for 5 more minutes; add water to adjust the consistency. Add salt if needed.
- Serve hot with rice, roti, or bread.

Nimbu Mirchi Salmon

(Chilli Lime Salmon)

 40 minutes | Serves  4

INGREDIENTS

4 salmon fillets, cut into 200 gm portions

3 tbsps olive oil

4 tbsps lemon juice

1 tsp chilli powder

1 tsp black pepper powder

1 tsp ginger paste

Salt to taste

IN A NUTSHELL

Simple, quick and delicious, Nimbu Mirchi Salmon brings together the spice, tang and zest seamlessly. An impressive main apt for a dinner party, it is appetising and healthy.

METHOD

- In a mixing bowl, add 2 tbsp olive oil, lemon juice, chilli powder, black pepper powder, ginger paste, and season it with salt.
- Add the salmon fillet and rub the fish with the marinade. Cover with cling flim and set aside in a cool place for 30 minutes.
- Preheat the oven and line the baking tray with paper. Place the fillet in the tray and bake for 12 minutes. Or, heat the residual oil in a pan and fry the salmon for a minute on each side.
- Serve with a nice tropical salad of your choice.

THE
POT-SHOT!!

Phanna Upkari

(Mangalorean Fish Curry)

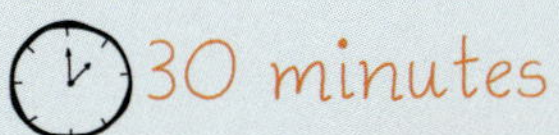

Serves

IN A NUTSHELL

A popular dish of the Konkani GSB community, Phanna Upkari is a delicious fish curry with a coconut base. It is a delicately spiced fish cooked in dense gravy with a coconut base that seamlessly brings together all the spices used. There isn't really a bad time to savour this curry, usually relished with steamed rice.

INGREDIENTS

4 mackerel fillets, about 200 gm each

Salt to taste

5 tbsps groundnut oil

½ tsp mustard seeds

½ tsp cumin seeds

½ tsp asafoetida

1 tsp ginger-garlic paste

3 medium-sized onions

1 tsp red chilli powder

1 ping-pong sized ball of tamarind, made into pulp.

½ cup warm water

Coriander to garnish (optional)

2 tbsps fresh coconut, grated

FOR MASALA:

½ tsp coriander seeds

12 red chillies

2 tsps tamarind pulp

2 tbsps fresh grated coconut

METHOD

- Rinse the fish, rub in a pinch of salt and keep aside.
- Heat ½ tsp oil in a small skillet. Add ingredients listed under masala i.e coriander seeds, red chillies, tamarind pulp and coconut until the ingredients amalgamate.
- Heat oil in a saucepan; splutter mustard seeds followed by cumin seeds and asafoetida.
- Add ginger-garlic paste with onion. Sauté until the onions start to caramelise.
- Add the coconut-spice paste and red chilli powder to the pan and sauté until the flavours start coming together in the pan for 5 minutes.
- Add fish and let it cook in the spices for about 1 minute. Stir occasionally. Season with salt. Keep in mind we've already rubbed some salt in the fish.
- Add tamarind pulp and water. Simmer until the curry reaches a desired consistency.
- Turn off the heat, garnish with coriander and serve hot with rice.

Prawn and Raw Mango Curry

40 minutes | Serves 2

IN A NUTSHELL

Inspired by the Malabar Coast, this Prawn and Raw Mango Curry is a comforting tangy curry that sets the mood for the perfect summer lunch. Dense, subtle and balanced, relish it with rice or roti.

INGREDIENTS

- 300 gm king prawns, shelled & deveined with tail left on
- 1 tbsp ginger paste
- 6 garlic cloves
- ¼ tsp turmeric powder
- 1 cup/200 ml water
- 3 tbsps vegetable oil
- 10 curry leaves
- ½ cup white onion, thinly sliced
- 1 green chilli, slit lengthwise
- ⅓ cup tomato, finely chopped
- 1 tsp kashmiri chilli powder
- 1 tbsp coriander powder
- 1 tbsp tomato puree
- 250 g raw mango chopped in chunks
- Pinch of sugar
- Salt to taste
- 50 ml coconut milk

METHOD

- Marinate the prawns with a paste of ginger, garlic, turmeric and 1 tsp water. Let it stay for about 30 minutes.
- Heat oil in a heavy bottom sauce pan over a medium flame. Splutter half the curry leaves and add the sliced onion and sauté over a medium heat for 7 minutes until it starts to turn translucent.
- Add the slit green chilli along with the chopped tomatoes and fry for 6 minutes.
- Soften the tomatoes well; add the powdered spices and tomato puree. Stir well mixing the spices and cooking them for a minute.
- Add the chopped raw mango and water. Bring to a boil and simmer.
- Add the sugar, salt stir well and simmer on a low heat for 2 minutes.
- Add the prawns and simmer the curry for 5 minutes with the lid on until the prawns are just cooked.
- Stir in the coconut milk and add the remaining curry leaves; simmer for 2 minute until the gravy thickens and the prawns are cooked through.
- Turn off the heat and set aside. Serve hot with roti or rice.

Maharashtrian Prawn Pulao

40 minutes | Serves  4

INGREDIENTS

20 prawns, peeled and deveined

1 ball of tamarind or 15 units of kokum

3 tsps red chilli powder

1 ½ tsps turmeric powder

1 tsp cumin powder

½ tsp asafoetida powder

2 ½ tsps ginger-garlic paste

1 cup rice

1 tbsp oil

2 bay leaves

5 black peppercorns

3 cloves

1 inch-long cinnamon stick

1 pod cardamom

1 large onion, finely chopped

1 tsp garam masala

2 green chillies, bilaterally slit and deseeded

1 tsp cumin seeds

1 tsp coriander powder

½ tsp goda masala (optional)

2 cups water

1 tsp ghee (clarified butter) (optional)

Salt to taste

METHOD

- Soak tamarind in warm water for about 15 minutes. Extract the pulp and put it through a strainer.
- Rinse the prawns and transfer to a large mixing bowl.
- Add ½ tsps of each – red chilli, turmeric, cumin and asafoetida powder, and ginger-garlic paste. Mix well gently, cover with cling film and leave to marinate in a cool place for 30 minutes.
- Rinse and drain the rice. Soak in cold water for about 20 minutes.
- Heat oil in a saucepan. Add bay leaves, black peppercorns, cloves, cinnamon and cardamom. Fry the spices until the flavours merge with the oil.
- Add the onions and sauté until transparent. Add the residual ginger-garlic paste along with the slit green chillies. Sauté for one more minutes.
- Add the residual turmeric, red chilli, cumin, and coriander powder. Follow this by adding tamarind pulp, garam masala and goda masala. Sauté and mix well until the spices come together in the pan.
- Add the marinated prawns and sauté for 3 minutes. Stir occasionally to make sure the protein doesn't stick to the bottom of the pan.
- Drain the pre-soaked rice to the saucepan and mix well.
- Add 2 cups of water and bring to a boil on high heat. Lower the heat to medium high and cook for 5 minutes and on low heat for another 10-15 minutes until the water evaporates.
- Remove from heat, keep covered and let it sit for 5 minutes.
- Serve hot with a dollop of ghee.

IN A NUTSHELL
Inspired from a Konkani grandma's age-old, Maharashtrian Prawn Pulao is aromatic, easy and quick to make. This flavourful rice dish is usually savoured piping hot with a dollop of ghee perched atop a mound of pulao on a languid Sunday.

Prawn Balchao

Serves

IN A NUTSHELL

An inheritance of the Catholic Portuguese settlers in the sushegado state, Balchao is a method used to preserve meat, usually fish. Fiery, tangy and sour, you can savour it as a pickle or make a curry out of it and relish it with rice.

INGREDIENTS

500 gms prawns, shelled and deveined

Salt as required

½ tsp turmeric powder

3 tbsps cooking oil

2 tbsps vinegar

5 cloves of garlic, finely sliced

1 inch ginger

8 curry leaves (optional)

1 medium-sized onion, finely chopped

1 tbsp sugar

BALCHAO PASTE:

10 Kashmiri red chillies

5 Byadgi red chillies, dried

½ tsp cumin seeds

1 tsp black peppercorn

6 cloves of garlic

5 cloves, whole

1 inch-long cinnamon stick

Vinegar as required

METHOD

- In a mixing bowl, add prawns and rub them with a tsp of salt and ½ tsp of turmeric powder. Set aside for half an hour.
- Heat oil in a fryer and fry the prawns until the shellfish turns brown. Remove from heat and sprinkle with a little vinegar. Set aside for an hour.
- Grind the Kashmiri and Byadgi red chillies, cumin seeds, black peppercorn, garlic, cloves and cinnamon into a fine paste. Use vinegar to adjust the consistency.
- Heat the oil used to deep fry the prawns in a pan and sauté garlic, ginger and curry leaves for 30 seconds.
- Add the onion and fry until translucent.
- Stir in the Balchao paste and sauté for 4 minutes.
- Add prawns and cook for 5 minutes until the masala thickens. Follow this by adding sugar and salt to adjust the sweet-tangy flavours.
- If you want to eat it as a curry, take the desired quantity aside and add water. Simmer until it reaches the desired consistency. If not, secure it in a liquid proof jar and mature for a period of 5-6 days.

Sukka Clams

40 minutes | Serves 4

IN A NUTSHELL

Inspired from the western Karnataka coast, this recipe features tamarind paste and coconut, two signature ingredients of the coast. Slightly dense, this curry is ideally mopped up with bread or roti.

INGREDIENTS

1 kg clams with shells
4 tbsps grated coconut
½ onion, roughly chopped
2 cloves garlic
1 tsp ginger
1 tsp tamarind paste
2 tbsps vegetable oil
¼ tsp mustard seeds
2-3 sprigs curry leaves
½ onion, finely sliced
Salt to season

FOR COCONUT MIX:

1 tsp red chilli powder
¾ tsp coriander powder
½ tsp cumin powder
¼ tsp black pepper powder
¼ tsp turmeric powder

METHOD

- Clean the clams thoroughly under running water and ensure there is no sand in them. Immerse in water for about an hour to ensure no traces of sands are left.
- Dry roast grated coconut and chopped onions in a non-stick pan until light brown. Stir occasionally to ensure you don't burn it.
- Add the rest of the spice powder listed under the coconut mix list. Sauté on low heat for another 30 seconds. Cool the mixture.
- Grind the cool mix along with garlic, ginger and tamarind paste into a coarse paste.
- Heat oil in a saucepan and splutter the mustard seeds and curry leaves. Add sliced onions; sauté till the onions turn light brown.
- Add the ground masala and fry lightly on low heat for about 2 minutes.
- Add the clams and season with salt.
- Cook on low heat covered for a couple of minutes until the clams cook; add a bit of water if you wish to make it slightly saucy.
- Serve hot.

Tamarind Shrimp Curry

40 minutes | Serves 4-6

IN A NUTSHELL

An ode to the grandmothers of Goa, this Konkani curry is inspired by the cuisine of the western coast of India. The tangy tamarind is balanced with soothing coconut milk and green chillies add the much-needed spice to this well-balanced curry. Relish this with piping hot steamed rice and let it take you to the land of Susegad – Goa!

INGREDIENTS

½ kg shrimp, peeled and deveined

Salt to taste

1 ½ tbsps lemon juice

¼ inch ginger, finely chopped

4-5 cloves of garlic, finely chopped

5 green chillies, finely chopped and deseeded

2 medium-sized onions, finely chopped

¾ cup coconut, freshly grated

1 ping-pong sized ball of tamarind

1 cup warm water

2 tbsps oil

1 tsp cumin seeds

½ tsp asafoetida,

½ tsp turmeric powder

1 tsp red chilli powder

Water as required

METHOD

- Rinse the shrimp in cold water. Sprinkle salt and lemon juice. Cover with a cling film and set aside to marinate for about 30 minutes.
- Make a fine, thick paste of ginger, garlic, green chillies and half of the onions.
- Run the grated coconut through the grinder until it makes a fine paste. Add ¼ cup water if necessary.
- Place the coconut paste in a clean, dry muslin cloth and squeeze out the coconut milk.
- Soak the tamarind in warm water and squeeze out pulp 10 minutes after it soaks.
- Heat oil in a saucepan on low heat.
- Splutter cumin seeds and add asafoetida.
- Add the rest of the onions and fry until transparent.
- Add the coconut paste with chillies in it and turmeric powder. Sauté for a couple of minutes.
- Add red chilli powder and tamarind pulp. Mix well.
- Add shrimps and cook with the lid on for 2 minutes. Follow this by adding coconut milk.
- Add a little water to adjust the consistency and simmer for another 5-8 minutes.
- Serve hot with rice or roti.

Sanpiau

Serves 

IN A NUTSHELL

Perhaps a dish that symbolises the North Eastern state of Mizoram, Sanpiau is both a delicacy relished at home and a street style snack. Fit for a comfort food craving, this humble dish comes close to the South East Asian congee – rice porridge spiced with regionally available condiments.

INGREDIENTS

1 cup short grain rice
3 cups fish stock
2 tsps garlic, finely chopped
Salt to taste
1 tbsp fish sauce
2 tbsps onion, crispy fried
2 tbsps green spring onions
½ tsp black pepper powder

METHOD

- Rinse and drain the rice. Soak in water for about 20 minutes. Drain and set aside.
- Use a cooker, crockpot, or a heavy bottom saucepan to heat the stock and add the rice. Cook with the lid on. Stir occasionally to ensure the mix doesn't stick to the bottom.
- Add garlic once the rice is almost cooked and season with salt.
- Ladle the rice porridge to serving bowls.
- Garnish with fish sauce, crispy onion, spring onions and black pepper powder. Serve hot.

Prawns Pullimunchi

30 minutes | Serves 3

THE POT-SHOT!!

IN A NUTSHELL

Hailing from the coastal state of Karnataka, Prawns Pullimunchi is a tangy, spicy dish that features the use of native byadgi chillies. These are easily substituted by paprika, habanero or cayenne peppers. You could make this into a curry and relish it with roti or rice or simmer this until it is dense and serve it atop bruschetta or canapés to make an ideal appetiser or bar grub.

INGREDIENTS

500 gms medium-sized shrimp, peeled and deveined

Salt to taste

½ tsp turmeric powder

1 lime sized ball of tamarind

10 dried byadgi chillies (in lieu of these you could use paprika or kundapura chillies)

2 green chillies, deseeded

7 garlic cloves

2 whole cloves

½ tsp mustard seeds

1 tsp cumin seeds

1 tbsp cooking oil

1 tsp garlic paste

METHOD

- Rinse the prawns under running water. Sprinkle salt and turmeric powder, cover and set aside for further use.
- Soak tamarind in warm water. Allow it to sit for 10 minutes and extract the pulp.
- Grind byadgi and green chillies, whole garlic cloves, whole cloves, and mustard and cumin seeds, and into a fine paste. Add the tamarind pulp to adjust the consistency.
- Heat oil in a saucepan to a smoking point.
- Lower the heat and fry garlic paste for 1 minute.
- Add prawns and let them fry on low flame for 4-5 minutes.
- Add the masala paste made earlier and mix well. Cook until the aroma starts wafting.
- Add a desired amount of water and simmer for not more than 5 minutes or until it reaches the desired consistency.
- Serve hot with rice or roti.

My Desi Fish N Chips

IN A NUTSHELL

Quick and easy, Fish N Chips is a classic that gets a desi makeover with the use of Indian spices. It makes for a great snack or even a meal for when you want to eat light. It is ideal for when you are in the mood to cook something simple or when you want to spend the night indoors while binge watching your favourite show.

INGREDIENTS

250 gms parboiled potatoes, cut into wedges

Salt to taste

¼ cup besan (chickpea flour)

½ tsp carom seeds

½ tsp turmeric powder

1 tsp red chili powder

½ tsp garam masala powder

⅓ cup lager beer (any commercially available beer)

250 gm fish fillets of your choice

¼ cup refined flour

½ tbsp refined oil

1 tsp lemon juice

2 slices lemon

METHOD

- Fry the potato wedges in hot oil until brown and crispy. Season with salt and red chilli powder.
- In a large mixing bowl, add the chickpea flour, carom seeds, turmeric powder, red chilli powder, garam masala powder, lager and salt.
- Pat the fish fillets dry and sprinkle all purpose flour over them coating lightly it on all sides.
- Heat oil in the deep fryer.
- Dip the fish in the the batter and ensure it's coated well. Put it into the fryer.
- Fry until it's olden brown and crisp on the outside.
- Transfer to a plate and dab the excess oil with a paper towel. Sprinkle lime juice.
- Repeat the process with the potato wedges.
- Serve hot with ranch or the delicious mint and green chilli chutney and lemon slices.

S. E. RAILWAY TENDER

Goan Mussels Xinaneao Fry

30 minutes | Serves 2

IN A NUTSHELL

Quick, simple and easy Xinaneao Fry hails from the coastal state of Goa. Mussels coated in the spices are shallow fried until crispy. These make for an impressive hors d'oeuvres served atop canapés or bruschetta.

INGREDIENTS

450 gms mussels, cleaned (refer step 1 of the method)

Water as needed

½ tsp ginger-garlic paste

½ tsp turmeric powder

1 tsp red chilli powder

½ tsp garam masala powder

Salt to taste

Oil to fry

½ cup semolina

½ tsp lemon juice

METHOD

- Clean the mussels under running water and let them sit in boiling water to ensure that they open. Clean the bear and the veins. Once opened, scoop them out with a spoon.
- Transfer them to a large mixing bowl.
- Add ginger-garlic paste, turmeric powder, red chilli powder, garam masala powder and salt. Cover it and put it in a cool place to marinade for about 45 minutes.
- Heat oil in a pan.
- In another bowl, add semolina and coat the mussels in it.
- Shallow fry in a pan until golden brown on both sides.
- Remove from heat and pat with a paper towel.
- Sprinkle lemon juice and serve hot with a side salad.

Prawn Ghee Roast

Serves 

IN A NUTSHELL

Aromatic and spicy, Prawn Ghee Roast hails from Mangalore, a town in Karnataka. As a dish that has acquired quite a following, it is easily available in most metros in India, but the perfect ghee roast, Mangaloreans believe is made at home. Pair this fiery aromatic dish with ghee, rice, biryani or a bread of your choice.

INGREDIENTS

250 gms prawns, cleaned and deveined cleaned and deveined

2 tbsps cooking oil

1 medium-sized onions, julienned

1 tsp turmeric powder

1 tsp red chilli powder

3 tbsps water

6 tsps ghee

2 sprigs of curry leaves

Salt to taste

FOR MASALA PASTE:

2 tomatoes, roughly chopped

7 cloves garlic

1 inch piece of ginger

2 tsps black pepper

1 tsp fennel seeds

METHOD

- Grind the ingredients listed under masala paste into a fine paste and set aside.
- Heat oil in a heavy bottom saucepan. Add onions and sauté until they are transparent.
- Add ground masala, turmeric powder, red chilli powder and water. Cover the pan and cook until the oil starts separating from the spices. Remove from heat, set aside.
- In the same saucepan, melt 3 tsps ghee and let the curry leaves splutter.
- Add prawns followed by the masala we had set aside earlier. Let it cook for 2 more minutes.
- Add the rest of the ghee, mix well and season with salt.
- Sauté until the prawns have cooked. Ensure the masala is dense enough for the prawns and not runny.
- Serve hot with appam, parotta, or savour as it is.

Amritsari Fish Fry

30 minutes | Serves 

IN A NUTSHELL

Delicious and delicately spiced fish fritters perhaps best describes Amritsari Fish Fry. It hails from the namesake city in Punjab and makes for a delicious snack or perhaps an appetiser for a dinner party. Savour it with a dip of your choice or staple mint-coriander green chutney.

INGREDIENTS

2 ½ cups salmon, cut into fingers
Salt to taste
3 tbsps ginger-garlic paste
1 tbsp red chilli powder
1 tsp carom seeds
1 tsp cumin powder
1 tsp raw mango powder
½ tsp coriander powder
1 cup besan or gram
Oil to deep fry
1 egg, whisked
1 tsp chaat masala
1 tbsp lemon juice

METHOD

- In a large mixing bowl, add the fish, salt and ginger-garlic paste. Let it rest for 10 minutes in a cool place.
- Add red chilli powder, carom seeds, salt, cumin powder, raw mango powder, coriander powder and gram flour. Mix well and ensure the powders have coated the fish on all sides.
- Heat oil in the deep fryer.

- Add the whisked egg and mix well.
- Gently release the fish into the fryer and fry until golden brown.
- Remove and place on or pat dry with a paper towel.
- Sprinkle the chaat masala and lemon juice.
- Serve hot with a side salad and a dip of your choice.

THE POT-SHOT!!

salt

Whole Baked Masala Snapper

40-50 minutes | Serves 2-3

IN A NUTSHELL

An impressive main dish, Baked Masala Snapper is appetising and rich in flavour. Blended perfectly with authentic spices and flavour, this dish is simple, delicious and easy to cook.

INGREDIENTS

Whole snapper fish, 1kg, cleaned and gutted
2 tbsp lemon juice

1 tsp turmeric powder/manjal podi salt

200 gm baby potatoes, parboiled and cut in half

FOR MASALA:

2 tbsp oil

A sprig of curry leaves

1 medium-sized onion, chopped

1 tbsp ginger-garlic paste

1 green chilli, finely chopped

½ tsp black pepper powder

1 tsp cumin powder

1 tbsp coriander powder

1 tsp fennel powder

1 tbsp red chilli powder

1 tbsp garam masala

2 tomatoes, finely chopped

Salt to taste

2 tbsp coriander leaves, finely chopped

2 tbsp mint leaves, finely chopped

METHOD

- Preheat oven to 220°C.
- Mix lemon juice and turmeric powder to a paste. Spread this all over and inside the fish and set aside.
- Heat oil in a pan. Add in curry leaves, onion and cook till golden.
- Add ginger-garlic paste, chillies and cook for a minute.
- Add all the spice powders and mix well.
- After that, add tomatoes, salt (as required) and cook till the tomatoes turn mushy.
- Finally, add coriander leaves and mint leaves. Mix well till the masala is done.
- Now line a foil, spoon some masala at the bottom. Lay the fish in, spoon some masala into the fish and over the fish. Lay down the cover and bake this for 30-35 minutes.
- Garnish with tomato slices and serve with steamed potato slices.

King Fish Curry

25 minutes | Serves  6–7

IN A NUTSHELL

The Indian subcontinent hosts a multitude of cuisines, so much so that even a simple fish curry has several variations considering the sheer amount of spices and ingredients available. This recipe brings together the slightly tangy raw mangoes and soothing coconut milk, giving it a distinctive flavour. Pair this with parotta and rice.

INGREDIENTS

1 kg king fish fillets, cut

3 tbsps coconut oil

¼ kg shallots, coarsely chopped

2 tbsps green chilli, chopped

3 tbsps ginger, chopped

1 tbsp turmeric powder

1 tbsp red chilli powder

1 medium-sized raw mango, diced

Salt to taste

15 curry leaves

2 cups coconut milk

Water as needed

METHOD

- Clean the fish under a gentle stream of water.
- Heat oil in a pan. then add shallots, green chilli and ginger. Sauté until the shallots soften.
- Add turmeric powder, red chilli powder and sauté for about 30 seconds.
- Add water and cook the masala for a minute.
- Add diced raw mango, salt and curry leaves. Add some more water if required and cook until the mangoes are soft.
- Add coconut milk and simmer on low heat. Add the fish to the simmering curry and allow it to cook for about 5 more minutes or until they are well done.
- Remove from heat and serve with steaming hot rice.

Machi Jaisamandi

45 minutes | Serves 2-3

INGREDIENTS

450 gms fish fillet of your choice

Salt to taste

Lemon juice to marinate

FOR THE BATTER:

4 tsp besan

¼ tsp turmeric powder

¼ tsp cumin powder

Water to make the batter

Oil to fry

FOR THE GREEN CHUTNEY:

½ cup coriander leaves

¼ cup mint leaves

1 green Chilli

½ tsp lemon juice

FOR THE GRAVY:

½ cup fresh cream

1 cup curd

¾ tsp turmeric powder

¼ tsp red chilli powder

¼ tsp cumin seeds

2 tsp cooking oil

Salt to taste

IN A NUTSHELL

Unlike usual fish curries, Machi Jaisamandi has the fish and the curry cooked separately and served together. This recipe hails from the royal kitchens of Rajasthan. One of the lesser known gems of this cuisine, this light subtly flavoured curry goes well with rice, roti, or any flatbread of your choice.

METHOD

- Wash the fish under a gentle stream of water, pat dry and rub in salt. Allow it to rest for 10 minutes.
- Grind the ingredients listed under green chutney into a fine paste, use water to adjust the quantity if required. Set aside for further use.
- In a large bowl, mix all the ingredients listed under the batter. Ensure that no lumps are formed. Set aside for further use.
- In another large bowl, add the ingredients listed under gravy except the oil and cumin seeds. Set aside.
- Take a piece of fish and apply chutney; repeat this with rest of the pieces and make pairs out of them placing the chutney side in the middle.
- Heat oil in a saucepan.
- Dip the fish fillet sandwich in the batter and shallow fry the fish for a minute on each side. Set aside.
- In the same pan add more oil (if required) splutter cumin seeds.
- Add the gravy mix made earlier along with the salt and bring to a boil. Turn off the heat.
- In the serving dish place the fried fish fillets and ladle the gravy on it.
- Serve hot with a bread of you choice and a crisp salad or raita.

Apollo Fish Fry

Serves 

IN A NUTSHELL

A popular bar snack and a delicious appetiser, Apollo Fish Fry hails from Hyderabad. It is not unusual to find this on the menus in most restaurants. This fish fry makes for a scrumptious appetiser by itself or when placed in canapés or a snack. It pairs best with a chilled pint of beer or two!

INGREDIENTS

750 gms fish fillet, boneless, cut into smaller pieces

½ tbsp turmeric powder

Salt to taste

1 tbsp red chilli powder

2 tsps coriander powder

⅓ tbsp ginger-garlic paste

Oil for fry

1 tbsp cornstarch

1 egg, whisked

½ inch ginger finely chopped

2 cloves garlic, finely chopped

A sprig of curry Leaves

4-5 green chillies, sliced

1 tbsp chilli sauce

1 tbsp soy sauce

½ cup curd

2 tsps black pepper powder

METHOD

- Clean the fish under running running water and drain.
- In a large mixing bowl, add fish, turmeric powder, salt, red chilli powder, coriander powder, ginger-garlic paste. Cover and let it sit for 20 minutes.
- Heat oil in a wok.
- Add cornstarch and whisked egg to the marinated fish. Mix well to ensure the egg-flour mix has coasted all the fish.
- Gently let the fish in the fryer and fry for 4-5 minutes or until golden brown. Remove from heat, dab with a paper towel and keep aside.
- In the same wok, add a little more oil if required. Add chopped ginger and garlic, sauté until the aroma wafts.
- Add curry leaves and chopped green chillies, sauté for a minute and stir in the chilli sauce followed by soy. Let it fry on a medium high heat for about a minute.
- Reduce the heat to low and add cornstarch, curd and black pepper powder to it. Ensure it mixes uniformly; sauté for about ½ minute.
- Add fried fish, increase the heat and stir fry until the ingredients mix well.
- Serve hot.

Bihari Fish Curry

Serves 

INGREDIENTS

750 gms rohu or any freshwater fish on the bone

Salt to taste

1 tbsp turmeric powder

5 tbsps mustard oil

1 bay leaf

½ cup onion paste

1 tbsp ginger-garlic paste

½ tbsp coriander powder

½ tbsp cumin powder

½ tbsp black pepper powder

½ tbsp yellow mustard paste

1 cup mix of veggies of your choice

½ tbsp red chilli powder

Water as needed

METHOD

- Clean the fish under the gentle stream of running water. Rub in some salt and 1 tsp of turmeric powder. Set aside for 20 minutes.
- Heat oil in a saucepan and shallow fry the marinated fish for about 1 minute on each side. Remove from heat, dab with a paper towel and set aside for further use.
- Add bay leaf, onion and ginger-garlic paste, and sauté for 2 minutes.
- Add coriander powder, cumin powder, black pepper, red chilli powder and turmeric powder along with the mustard paste and sauté for 2 minutes.
- Add the vegetables, sauté for 2 more minutes. Cover and cook until the vegetables have semi-cooked.
- Use a spatula to move the vegetables to the side exposing the bottom of the pan.
- Add the fish in the centre of the pan. Mix well.
- Add water as required and bring to a boil on medium low heat. Check for the salt and season if required.
- Reduce the heat to low, cover and simmer until the gravy reaches the desired consistency. Remove from heat.
- Serve hot with rice.

IN A NUTSHELL

This Magadhi cuisine, better known as Bihari cuisine is one of the lesser known throughout the Indian subcontinent. Bihari Fish Curry is a simple fish curry that hails from the northern state of Bihar. It is quick and easy to make with fiery mustard paste for the base and is often paired with rice.

Daab Chingri

40 minutes | Serves 

IN A NUTSHELL

Loosely translated to pressure shrimp, Daab Chingri is a delicious curry from the Bengali cuisine. A festive speciality, it is made especially for Durga Puja. This curry features an amalgamation of mustard and coconut milk. It is best relished with a piping hot pile of rice.

INGREDIENTS

½ kg prawns, shelled and deveined

3 medium-sized tender coconuts

Salt to taste

1 ½ tsp turmeric powder

1 ½ tbsp mustard seeds

4 green chilies, finely chopped

2 ½ tsp ginger-garlic paste

5 tbsp mustard oil

6 tbsp onion paste

1 bay leaf

2 tsp red chilli powder

½ tsp sugar

3 tsp garam masala powder

METHOD

- Make a slight cut at the base of the coconut so that it can stand. Make another round incision on the top and keep the cutout flap for later use.
- Drain the coconut water (retain it for later use) and scoop out the flesh in two different bowls.
- Rinse the prawns with cold water, rub in a little salt and ½ tsp turmeric powder. Cover it with cling film and set aside for about half an hour.
- Grind the grated coconut, tender coconut flesh, mustard seeds, green chillies, and ginger-garlic paste into a fine smooth paste. Add coconut water to adjust the consistency.
- Grind onions into a fine paste, use plain water to get the desired consistency.
- Heat oil in a saucepan and lightly sear the prawns on both sides for about 30 seconds on low flame; take if off the heat.
- Heat oil in the same saucepan, add the bay leaf and let it fry for 30 seconds.
- Follow this by adding the onion paste and fry until the onions start caramelising.
- Add the garam masala powder and let it cook until the aroma wafts.
- Add coconut paste and let it cook with the lid until the ingredients come together.
- Add red chilli powder, turmeric, and sugar. Mix well until this base of the curry starts releasing some fat from the body.
- Add the coconut water and lightly sear the prawns. Bring it to a boil over low heat and add coconut milk.
- Pour this cooked curry in the tender coconut, then place the circular flap over it so to seal it.
- Preheat the microwave at 180°C, cook further for 20 minutes. Or, place the tender coconut in a pressure cooker submerged halfway in water.
- Secure the lid of the pressure cooker and cook further for 10 minutes.
- Serve hot with piping hot rice or luchi with a wedge of Gondhoraj lemon.

Mackerel Masala Fry

30 minutes | Serves 2

IN A NUTSHELL

Mackerel is a commonly available saltwater fish with a high nutritional value. This spicy mackerel fry is a quick and simple recipe for when you want to stay in. Relish it with roti, rice, or as is perhaps with a salad.

INGREDIENTS

2 whole mackerel, about 400g each (guts removed and cleaned)

1 tsp black peppercorns

1 tsp chilli powder

1 tsp cumin seeds

1 tsp coriander seeds

½ tsp turmeric powder

1 lemon, juiced

½ tsp ginger-garlic paste

1 tbsp vegetable oil

Salt to taste

METHOD

- Dry roast black peppercorns, chilli powder, cumin seeds, coriander seeds for 5 minutes in a pan.
- Cool the mix, add turmeric, juice of one lemon, ginger-garlic paste, salt and grind into a smooth paste.
- Slit the fish across the body and marinade with the spice paste. Cover and keep aside in a cool place for about 30 minutes.
- Heat oil in a shallow pan on low heat and place the fish on it.
- Let the fish fry on both the sides for about 8 to 10 minutes.
- Transfer to a plate and serve hot with a crisp salad.

Pomfret Moilee

Serves 

IN A NUTSHELL

Moilee is a staple curry from the southern most state, Kerala. This creamy, comforting curry has a coconut milk base and amalgamates spices brought to the Malabar Coast by the traders and merchants. It makes for a good curry on a cold night and it pairs best with steaming hot rice along with poppadoms on the side.

INGREDIENTS

6 small pomfrets (200 gms each), cleaned and gutted. Or 6 fillets (150 gms each)

½ tsp turmeric powder

1 tsp black pepper powder

1 tbsp lime juice

2 tbsp coconut oil

½ tsp mustard seeds

1 medium-sized onion, chopped

3 whole cardamoms

1 inch ginger, finely chopped

5 garlic cloves, finely chopped

½ tsp fenugreek seeds, crushed

2 sprigs curry leaves

4 green chillies, deseeded and finely chopped

1 small tomato, chopped

1 tsp coriander powder

1 cup coconut milk

Salt to taste

METHOD

- Wash the fish under a gentle stream of running water. Set aside.
- In a large mixing bowl add the fish, turmeric powder, pepper powder, lime juice, and coconut oil. Mix well, cover and set aside in a cool place.
- Heat 1 tbsp oil in a saucepan and add the marinated fish. Fry on both sides for about 1 minute on each side. Remove from heat and set aside.
- Add the rest of the oil in the same pan. Splutter mustard seeds.
- Add onion, cardamom, ginger and garlic, fenugreek seeds, curry leaves, and green chillies. Sauté the spices until the aromas start wafting.
- Add tomato and sauté until they cook. Add coriander and pepper powder, followed by half cup of the coconut milk. Bring it to a boil on medium heat.
- Reduce the heat and add the fish. Let it simmer for about 2 minutes then add the rest of the milk.
- Simmer for 2 more minutes or until the curry reach the desired consistency. Remove from heat.
- Serve hot with rice or parotta, and a crisp salad of your choice.

THE POT-SHOT!!

Squid Pepper Fry

Serves 4

IN A NUTSHELL

A popular appetiser, Squid Pepper Fry hails from the lush southern state of Kerala. Calamari or squids are sautéed in a dense, delicious ensemble of spices to make this delicious side dish or appetiser. It pairs well with a crisp lager making it a popular bar grub.

INGREDIENTS

- ½ kg squid, cut into rings
- 2 tsp red chilli powder
- ½ tsp turmeric powder
- Salt to taste
- 1 tsp ginger-garlic paste
- 1 ½ tsp lemon juice
- 3 tbsp coconut oil
- 1 inch ginger
- 6-7 cloves of garlic
- 16-18 curry leaves
- 2 medium-sized onions, chopped
- 2 green chillies, slit and deseeded
- 2 medium-sized tomatoes, chopped
- ½ tsp black pepper powder
- Coriander leaves to garnish
- Lemon wedges for a side

METHOD

- In a large mixing bowl, add squid, red chilli powder, turmeric powder, salt, half of the ginger-garlic paste and lemon juice. Cover with cling film and set aside for 20 minutes.
- Heat 1 tbsp coconut oil in a pan, add ginger, garlic and sauté. Follow this by sputtering curry leaves.
- Add onions and green chillies, sauté for a minute.
- Add tomatoes and salt, cook covered until the tomatoes soften.
- In another pan, heat the rest of the coconut oil splutter curry leaves, and add marinated squids. Sauté on high heat until semi cooked.
- Add the masala from the other pan and mix well. Add the rest of the red chilli powder, sprinkle some water.
- Cover and cook until the squids cook. Remove from heat and add lemon juice and pepper powder.
- Garnish with lemon wedges and coriander leaves. Serve hot.

Malabar Fish Curry

IN A NUTSHELL

Malabar coast is located in the south western state of Kerala. The cuisine is robust and the curry is flavourful. Fit for a languid meal, serve it with rice and pappadam, perhaps with pickle too.

INGREDIENTS

450 gms fish of your choice, cleaned and deboned

Salt to taste

3 tbsp coconut oil

¼ tsp fenugreek seeds

1 medium-sized onion, julienned

3 dried red chillies, whole

2 green chillies, deseeded and finely chopped

1 medium-sized tomato, finely chopped

3 tsp garlic, finely chopped

2 tsp ginger, finely chopped

A sprig of curry leaves

2 tbsp tamarind paste

Water if required

FOR THE SPICE PASTE:

1 ¼ cup freshly grated coconut

¼ tsp turmeric powder

1 tsp red chilli powder

1 ½ tsp coriander powder

METHOD

- Gently rinse the fish under a stream of water, drain well. Rub salt and let it sit in a cool place for further use.
- Grind all the ingredients listed in the spice paste list into a fine paste, adjust consistency with water if required.
- Heat oil in a saucepan. Allow the oil to reach a smoking point on high heat. Once it reaches there, reduce the heat and crackle fenugreek seeds.
- Add onion and sauté until they look translucent.
- Add red and green chillies followed by garlic, ginger, and curry leaves. Sauté until the aroma of the spices starts wafting.
- Add tomato and cook covered until soft and pulpy.
- Add the spice paste made earlier. Sauté for about 2-3 minutes until the ingredients mix well.
- Add water and bring it to a boil on high heat. Lower heat and add the tamarind paste followed by the fish.
- Add water if required to adjust the consistency of the gravy. Simmer until the fish is cooked and the gravy has your desired consistency. Turn off the heat.
- Serve hot with rice, parotta, or appam.

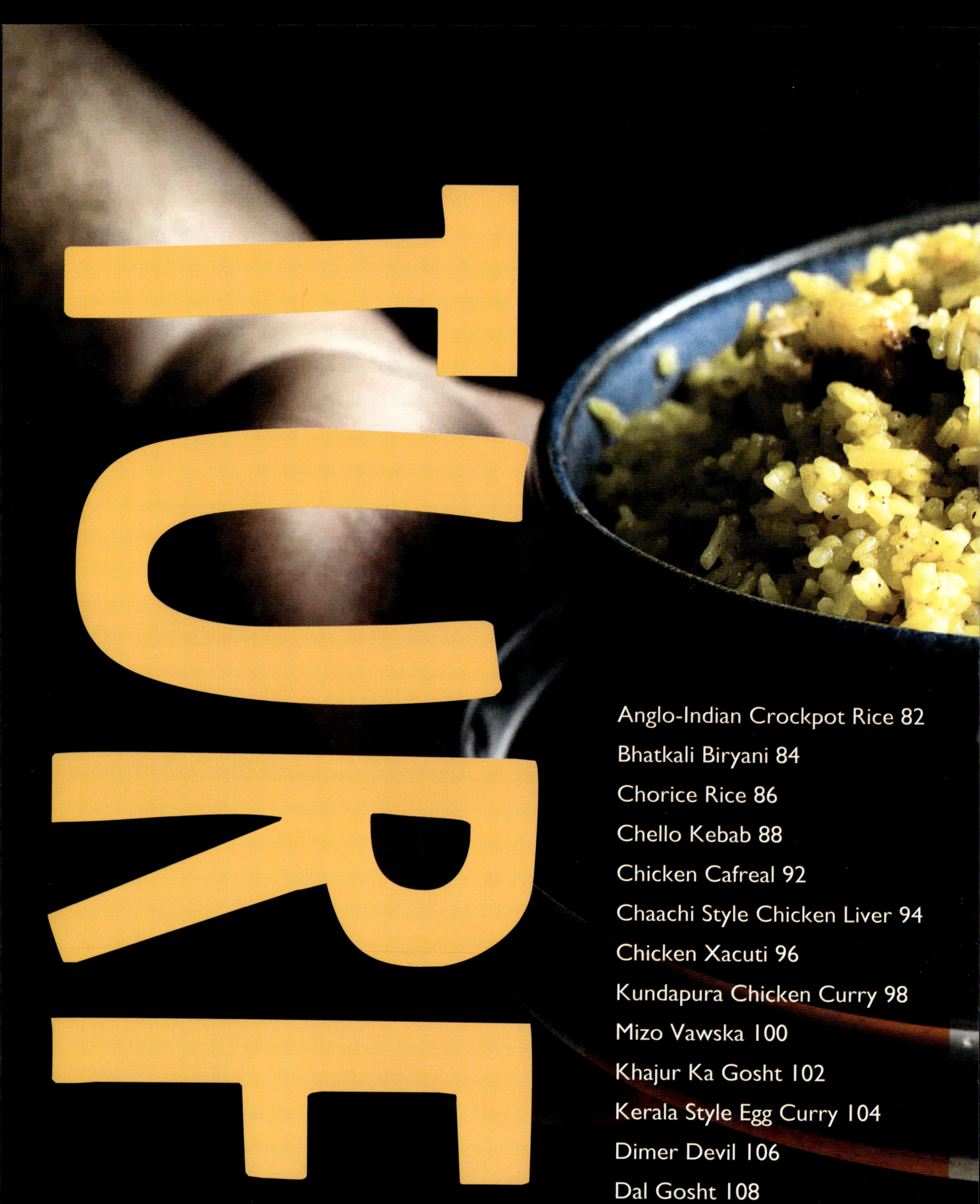

TURF

Anglo-Indian Crockpot Rice

30 minutes | Serves 4

IN A NUTSHELL

Quick and easy, this one pot wonder hails from the Anglo-Indian community. Comforting and delicious, the Anglo-Indian Crockpot Rice is perfect after a long day!

INGREDIENTS

½ kg chicken, boneless
2 cup basmati rice
Water as needed
2 tbsps butter, unsalted
2 tbsps canola oil
1 medium-sized onion, julienned
4 cloves garlic, whole crushed
2 inch ginger, minced
2 pods of cardamom, crushed
2 bay leaves
2 tsps black peppercorn, whole
Salt to taste
5 cups chicken stock
A sprig of mint leaves

METHOD

- Rinse and drain rice. Add water and soak for about an hour.
- Cut chicken into 1 inch cubes. Rinse, drain and set aside.
- In a saucepan, heat butter and oil together and sauté onions until translucent.
- Add garlic, half of the ginger, cardamom, bay leaves and peppercorn; sauté until the flavours start integrating into the oil. Stir often.
- Add the chicken and sauté until it is semi-cooked for about 4 minutes.
- Season with salt. Add rice and mix well with the spices and chicken.
- Add chicken stock, residual ginger and mint leaves. Simmer till it reaches porridge-like consistency.
- Serve hot!

THE POT-SHOTS!!

Bhatkali Biryani

INGREDIENTS

1 kg chicken

3 cups chicken stock 2 tbsps milk

1 tsp saffron

4 tbsps cooking oil

3 bay leaves

1 pod of green cardamom

1 inch-long cinnamon stick

4 cloves

2 medium-sized onions, chopped

¼ tsp turmeric powder

2 medium-sized tomatoes, julienned

2 tsps ginger-garlic paste

1 ½ cups coriander leaves, coarsely chopped

1 cup mint leaves, coarsely chopped

1 tbsp red chilli powder

8 green chillies, bilaterally slit

1 tbsp garam masala powder

Water as needed

2 cups basmati rice

1 tbsp lime juice

2 tbsps ghee

2 cups onions, caramelised

1 ping pong ball-sized ball of dough kneaded Salt to taste

IN A NUTSHELL

It is argued that biryani is a Persian import to India. Over the years, the dish has acquired several regional variations. The Indian subcontinent boasts of about 40 variations of biryanis, Bhatkali Biryani being one of them. This delicious biryani is the symbol of Bhatkali cuisine, a community native to Karnataka. It is arguably the most popular of the namesake cuisine found in the state.

120 minutes | Serves

METHOD

- Warm the milk and soak saffron in it.
- Heat 2 tbsps oil in a pot and add bay leaves, cardamom, cinnamon and cloves. Keep the heat on low until the spices start infusing in the oil.
- Sauté onions until transparent. Add turmeric powder followed by tomatoes. Sauté for until the tomatoes cook .
- Add ginger-garlic paste, coriander, mint leaves, chilli powder, green chillies, garam masala powder. Mix well. Sauté for 2 more minutes.
- Add the chicken with a cup of stock. Cook with the cover until the chicken starts to tenderise on a low flame.
- In another pot, add 2 cups water, rice, and 2 tbsps oil and bring to a boil.
- Semi-cook the rice and drain the water.
- Add the semi-cooked rice to the chicken along with saffron, lime juice and ghee.
- Pour over the chicken stock and cover the pot and top with caramelised onion.
- Seal with the dough and cook on low flame for about an hour.
- Serve hot with delicious raita.

Chorice Rice

20 minutes | Serves 2-3

IN A NUTSHELL

Simple and robust, this stir-fried rice is made with a handful of ingredients. A quick and convenient one pot wonder, the Goan fermented pork sausages as the star ingredient lends this dish a flavourful taste.

INGREDIENTS

2 cups Goan red rice, cooked
1 cup Goan chorice sausage
2 tbsps cooking oil
2 medium-sized onions, finely chopped
1 tsp ginger-garlic paste
½ tsp turmeric powder
¼ cup assorted bell peppers, sliced
1 cup button mushrooms, sliced
½ tsp black pepper powder
1 tsp red chilli powder (if needed)
3 cups basmati rice, cooked
Coriander to garnish (optional)
Salt to taste

METHOD

- Remove the sausage casing and chop the sausage coarsely.
- Heat oil in a skillet, add and sauté onions and ginger-garlic paste until the onions start to caramelise.
- Add turmeric powder along with the sausages. Sauté for 2 minutes.
- Add the bell peppers and sauté in the oil and lard until the bell peppers are semi-cooked.
- Add mushrooms and sauté for a minute or until they soften.
- Season with black pepper powder and red chilli powder. Sauté further for 2 minutes.
- Add the cooked rice and stir fry until the rice is ensconced in the flavours and spices in the pan.
- Serve hot.

Apple Mead

Chello Kebab

 90 minutes | Serves 

IN A NUTSHELL

A comforting dish brought to India by the merchants from Iran, these delicious meat kebabs are served on a bed of rice cooked in chicken stock. Relish this with wedges of lime that add a zesty flavour and a refreshing taste.

KEBAB:

2 medium-sized onions, pureed

2 garlic cloves

3 tbsps lemon juice

3 tbsps olive oil

Salt to taste

¼ tsp black peppercorns, powdered

1 kg lamb, boneless

18 cherry tomatoes

CHELLO:

2 cups basmati rice

1 cup warm water

6 cups chicken stock

Salt to taste

3 tbsps butter, unsalted

2 tbsps green onion, chopped

¼ tsp saffron, crushed

1 tbsp olive oil

2 tbsps mint leaves, chopped

1 tbsp coriander leaves, chopped

6 lemon wedges

METHOD

- In a large mixing bowl, add onions, garlic cloves, lemon juice, olive oil, salt and pepper.
- Add the mutton and marinade well. Cover with a cling film and set in the refrigerator for about 30 minutes
- Rinse and drain the rice with warm water. Keep aside.
- In a saucepan, add chicken stock and salt, and bring to a boil.
- Add rice and boil on medium heat uncovered for about a minute, stir occasionally.
- Drain the rice through a sieve into a bowl; retain both the rice and cooking liquid.
- In the same saucepan, add rice, butter, green onion, and saffron and cook over high heat.
- Add retained chicken stock. Add some more butter if required and cook for 5 minutes on high flame until the rice is cooked yet has some gravy.
- Put the lamb mince on skewers, dividing the kebabs with cherry tomatoes.
- Coat with cooking oil, and grill until they cook.
- Serve the kebabs on a bed of rice garnished with charred tomatoes, coriander leaves, mint, and lime wedges.

CARCEL DTTO JUDICIAL
MEDELLIN
128482

Chicken Cafreal

120 minutes | Serves 4-5

IN A NUTSHELL

Chicken Cafreal hails from the land of susegad Goa. Unlike other mains, this isn't a curry so dense that it sticks to the meat; Chicken Cafreal can either be served dry or with curry. Made with green chillies, coriander and vinegar, this exquisite dish which originally comes from the Portuguese colonies in Africa isn't for the faint hearted.

INGREDIENTS

1 kg chicken, curry cut on the bone
1 tbsp ginger-garlic paste
1 tbsp lime juice
Salt to taste
2 pods of green cardamom
1 inch ginger, roughly chopped
½ cup coriander leaves with the stem
1 tbsp coriander seeds
3 green chillies
8 cloves of garlic, coarsely chopped
5 cloves
½ tsp black peppercorn
½ cup tamarind pulp (or 1 tbsp vinegar)
½ inch-long cinnamon stick
½ tsp cumin seeds
1 tsp poppy seeds
2 tbsps cooking oil
1 cup chicken stock
2 tbsps vinegar

METHOD

- In a large mixing bowl add chicken, ginger-garlic paste, lime juice and salt. Cover with a cling film and marinate for about 60 minutes in the refrigerator.
- Grind cardamom, ginger, coriander leaves, coriander seeds, green chillies, garlic, cloves, peppercorns, tamarind pulp, cinnamon, cumin and poppy seeds into a smooth fine paste.
- Add this spice mix to the bowl and marinate the chicken for 30 minutes.
- Heat oil in the saucepan and add the chicken with the residual marinade.
- Cook with the lid on for 5 minutes.
- Add chicken stock and simmer until the chicken cooks entirely.
- Adjust the seasoning with vinegar and cook further till the gravy thickens and clings on to the meat.
- Serve hot with Goan sourdough or bread.

Chaachi Style Chicken Liver

Serves 

INGREDIENTS

1 kg chicken liver

Oil as needed

1 tsp mustard seeds

5-6 garlic cloves, finely chopped

5-6 curry leaves, chopped

2 medium-sized onions, chopped

4 tbsp fried onion and coconut paste

1 tsp turmeric powder

Salt as per taste

2 tsp red chili powder

2 tbsp tomato puree

Water as needed

2 green chillies, deseeded and finely chopped

Lemon juice to garnish

IN A NUTSHELL

Liver may not seem like the most appetising part of the chicken unless you're referring to this homestyle special recipe. Inspired by the regular household kitchens and the narrow by-lanes popular for peddling Ramadan delicacies, this recipe is an ode to them.

METHOD

- Heat oil in a pan and splutter mustard seeds.
- Add finely chopped garlic and curry leaves.
- Next, add onions and stir-fry till translucent.
- Add the fried onion and coconut paste and stir well till they blend well.
- Add turmeric powder, salt, red chili powder and stir well till the paste leaves out oil and turns brown.
- Add tomato puree and let it cook for about 3 minutes.
- Add chicken liver, water and cover and cook till done.
- Garnish with green chili and sprinkle lime juice. Serve hot with some onion and lemon rings.

Chicken Xacuti

50 minutes | Serves 4

INGREDIENTS

750 gms chicken, cut into small pieces on the bone

3 tbsps cooking oil

1 medium-sized onion, chopped

½ coconut, freshly grated

2 green chillies, slit

A sprig of curry leaves

2 cups chicken stock

Salt to taste

¼ cup coriander leaves, roughly chopped to garnish

Water as needed

FOR XACUTI:

2 tbsps cooking oil

1 ½ medium-sized onions, julienned

2 inch-long cinnamon stick

2 pods of green cardamom

8 cloves

1 tsp black peppercorns

2 tsps poppy seeds

¼ star anise

½ mace

1 tbsp coriander seeds

½ tsp nutmeg powder

5 Kashmiri red chilli dried

½ tsp turmeric powder

¼ aniseed

FOR GREEN MASALA:

¼ cup coriander leaves with the stem

12 cloves of garlic, coarsely chopped

2 green chillies, coarsely chopped

½ inch ginger, coarsely chopped

Salt to taste

METHOD

- Grind the ingredients in the green masala list into a fine paste; use water if required.
- Rinse the chicken in cold water and transfer it into a large mixing bowl.
- Marinate with the green masala paste and cover with cling film. Leave to marinate for at least 60 minutes.
- Heat 2 tbsps oil in a pan and sauté onions until transparent. Add coconut and sauté until the mix turns brown.
- Add all the ingredients listed under Xacuti masala and sauté for 3-5 minutes. Let it cool.
- Grind this sautéed spice into a fine paste; use water to adjust the consistency.
- Heat 3 tbsps oil in a saucepan and fry onions and green chillies. Follow this by sputtering the curry leaves.
- Add the marinated chicken to the pan and cook with the lid on for about 10 minutes.
- Add the Xacuti masala paste and cook for 10 minutes.
- Add chicken stock and cook until the meat is well-cooked. Add salt.
- Garnish with coriander leaves and serve hot with Goan sourdough bread or rice.

IN A NUTSHELL
A dense Goan curry cooked in a plethora of spices, Xacuti is a fiery, robust curry. This heavy curry dish is fit for a Sunday lunch because it lulls one into a deep slumber.

Kundapura Chicken Curry

30 minutes | Serves 4-6

IN A NUTSHELL

Kundapura Chicken Curry is native to the eponymous region in Karnataka, a place which has a culinary history of robust Indian spices. The use of coconut along with the spices is what gives this curry its distinct flavour. It is best relished with rice and bhakri, a cereal flatbread made in the rural Konkan coastal areas. This curry is light, delicious and comforting.

INGREDIENTS

1 kg chicken, curry cut with the bone

4 tbsps coconut oil

1 tsp cumin seeds

A sprig of curry leaves

¼ cup onions, chopped

¼ cup tomatoes, chopped

4 tsps ginger-garlic paste

1 cup chicken stock

Salt to taste

FOR KUNDAPURA PASTE:

7 cloves

1 tsp black peppercorn

1 tsp cumin seeds

1 inch-long cinnamon stick

2 tsps coriander seeds

5 red chillies

1 whole coconut, grated

1 cup chicken stock

METHOD

- Dry roast ingredients under the Kundapura Paste list and grind into a dense, fine paste. Use the chicken stock to adjust the consistency, if required. Set aside for later use.
- Heat coconut oil in a pan, splutter cumin seeds and curry leaves.
- Follow this by adding onions; sauté until translucent.
- Add tomatoes and ginger-garlic paste. Sauté until the onions start to caramelise and the tomatoes start peeling.
- Add the ground Kundapura paste sauté until the spices start to separate.
- Add chicken, use the chicken stock to adjust the consistency of this rather dense gravy. Add salt.
- Cover and cook until the chicken is well-cooked.
- Serve with piping hot rice and pickles.

Mizo Vawska

(Meghalaya Stir-fried Pork)

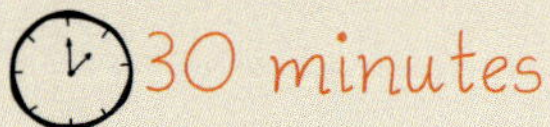

Serves 

IN A NUTSHELL

Simple, delicious and healthy, Mizo Vawska is a stir fried main hailing from the North Eastern state of Mizoram. Usually eaten as a main with a side of sticky rice, it also tastes delectable as it is.

300 gms smoked pork

1 inch piece of ginger, julienned

2 large cloves of garlic, crushed

1 tsp king chilli paste

1 cup oyster mushrooms

Salt to taste

1 green chilli, finely chopped

1 tsp oyster sauce (optional)

2 cups baby spinach

1 tsp black pepper powder (optional)

METHOD

- Slice the smoked pork thinly and then cut it into 2 cm strips after trimming the fat.
- Heat the lard in a pan and sauté ginger, garlic and king chilli paste for about 3 minutes.
- Add oyster mushrooms and a pinch of salt.
- Add smoked pork, chopped chillies, oyster sauce and some water (if needed). Cover and turn the heat to low.
- Simmer for another couple of minutes. Once the water evaporates, add baby spinach and stir until it wilts.
- Remove from heat, season with salt and black pepper.
- Serve with sticky rice.

Khajur Ka Gosht

 40 minutes | Serves  4-6

IN A NUTSHELL

Hailing from the royal kitchens of Awadh, Khajur Ka Gosht is a sweet and savoury meat curry made with dried dates. Lost in time and recently revived, this curry is hearty, wholesome, and makes for a regal yet comforting dish, best relished with naan or paratha.

INGREDIENTS

1 kg mutton, curry cut
Salt to taste
3 tbsps oil
2 bay leaves
3 medium-sized onions, finely chopped
1 tsp turmeric powder
½ cup cashew nut paste
1 cup water
2 cups dried dates
2 tbsps ginger-garlic paste
1 tsp red chilli powder
2 tsps coriander powder
½ tsp green cardamom powder
½ tsp garam masala powder
2 tbsps lemon juice
3 drops kewda water (fragrant floral water, optional)
1 tsp ghee

METHOD

- Rinse the meat thoroughly with water. Sprinkle some salt, cover and set aside.
- Heat 1 tbsp oil in a heavy bottom saucepan and add bay leaves.
- Add chopped onions and fry until the onions start to caramelise.
- Add turmeric, cashew paste, mutton and water. Season with salt. Place the lid on the pan and cook for the 10-15 minutes on medium high heat. Remove from heat and set aside.
- Grind the dates into a fine paste using water as needed, set aside for later use.
- Heat oil in another pan and add the ginger-garlic paste. Sauté for a minute.
- Add red chilli and coriander powder sauté for 2 minutes.
- Add the ground date paste followed by the precooked mix from the other saucepan. Mix well.
- Mix in green cardamom and garam masala powders, lemon juice and kewda water. Once the ingredients start cooking together, cook for 5 minutes without the lid, stir occasionally. Continue to cook with the lid on until the meat is cooked thoroughly.
- Add ghee and serve hot with rice or roti.

Kerala Style Egg Curry

IN A NUTSHELL

Hailing from the state of Kerala, this delicacy, the locals believe is a versatile curry. It can be eaten for breakfast, lunch or dinner. However, it is preferable for a dinner, especially on a night spent indoors.

 50 minutes | Serves 

INGREDIENTS

- 1 tbsp coconut oil
- ½ tsp mustard seeds
- 8 curry leaves
- 1 medium-sized onion, chopped
- 1 tsp ginger-garlic paste
- ½ tsp turmeric powder
- 2 green chillies, deseeded and slit
- 1 tsp garam masala powder
- ½ tsp black pepper, crushed
- 2 medium-sized tomatoes, finely chopped
- Salt to taste
- 2 cups coconut milk, freshly extracted
- 8 eggs, hard boiled

METHOD

- In a heavy bottomed pan, heat oil and splutter mustard seeds. Follow this by adding curry leaves.
- Sauté chopped onion, ginger-garlic paste, turmeric powder and green chillies until the onion starts to caramelise.
- Add garam masala with crushed black pepper. Sauté until the spices and flavours mix.
- Add tomatoes and cook with the lid on medium high heat for 2 minutes, stir occasionally. Add salt.
- Lower the heat and gently introduce the coconut milk. Bring to a simmer.
- Add the hardboiled eggs to the curry when it starts simmering. Cook for another 5 minutes.
- Serve hot with a bread, roti, rice, parotta or appam.

Dimer Devil

50 minutes | Serves  4

IN A NUTSHELL

A favourite Bengali street style snack, this is an adaptation of Scotch eggs, perhaps a hand-me-down from the British Raj. Usually served with a liberal amount of pungent kasundi (mustard), it is a hearty snack best relished in the monsoons and winters.

METHOD

- Mash the potatoes finely.
- Dry roast cumin and red chilli; grind them into a fine powder.
- Heat 2 tbsps oil in a pan. Add onion and garlic and fry until golden brown.
- Add garlic paste, red chilli, cumin, and turmeric powders. Sauté until the seasoning mixes well.
- Add the minced chicken and cook with the lid on until the meat is tender.
- Turn off the heat and let it cool.

INGREDIENTS

½ kg chicken, minced
2 medium-sized boiled potatoes
1 tsp cumin powder
2 tsps red chilli powder
Oil to fry
1 small onion, finely chopped
2 tsps garlic paste
5 red chillies, deseeded and finely chopped
1 tsp turmeric powder
3 green chillies, deseeded and chopped
Salt to taste
4 eggs, hard boiled
2 tbsps mustard oil
1 egg whisked
1 bowl of breadcrumbs
1 tsp chaat masala

- Fold green and red chillies and salt in mashed potatoes. Season with salt.
- Peel the hard boiled eggs and cut bilaterally into halves.
- Make tiny mounds of the potato mash to compliment the shape of bilaterally cut eggs.
- Press the egg and the potato mash mound together.
- Once the mince is cooled, gently press the mince around the egg and potato orb shaping it like a whole egg.
- Heat oil in a fryer on medium low heat.
- Give this sphere an egg wash, followed coating it with bread crumbs on all sides.
- Gently slide this into the fryer and fry until it acquires a shade of dark brown.
- Serve hot sprinkled with chaat masala and a side of kasundi relish.

Dal Gosht

55 minutes | Serves

2-3

IN A NUTSHELL

Similar to the Parsi Dhansak, Dal Gosht is a quick meat and lentil curry. A staple of the Bohri Muslim community, this curry is simple, easy to make and delicious, especially when relished with rice.

INGREDIENTS

500 gms mutton on the bone

2 cups of water

Salt to taste

2 tbsps ginger-garlic paste

2 tbsps cooking oil

1 tsp cumin seeds

1 bay leaf

5 cloves

2 star anise

1 pods garlic, chopped

1 medium-sized onion, finely chopped

1 medium-sized tomato, chopped

1 tsp turmeric powder

1 tsp garam masala powder

2 tsps Kashmiri red chilli powder

1 tsp jaggery sugar

¾ cup split pigeon peas, soaked overnight

3 cups mutton stock

¼ cup coriander, coarsely chopped

1 green chilli, chopped

1 tbsp lemon juice

METHOD

- Heat water in a heavy bottom pan. Add salt, ginger-garlic paste and mutton.
- Cook with the lid on until the mutton is semi-cooked. Set aside.
- Heat oil in a saucepan and sputter cumin seeds. Follow this with bay leaf, cloves, and star anise. Fry until the oil acquires the flavour of the spices.
- Add garlic and sauté for 3 minutes.
- Add onion and green chilli; sauté until transparent.
- Add tomato, turmeric, garam masala, and red chilli powder, and sauté until the tomato cooks.
- Add jaggery sugar and sauté until it mixes well with all ingredients stir continuously so that the sugar doesn't burn.
- Drain the lentil and add it to the pan along with mutton.
- Add 1 cup of the stock and bring to a boil on high heat.
- Reduce the heat, add the rest of the stock and adjust to the desired consistency.
- Simmer until the mutton is cooked. Add lime juice, mix well.
- Garnish with coriander and serve hot with rice.

Gondhoraj Lemon Chicken

70 minutes | Serves 4

IN A NUTSHELL

A Bengali classic, Gondhoraj Lemon Chicken is natively known as Lebu Lonka Murgi. The highlight of this dish is the citrusy eponymous lemon native to the Bengal delta and lends the flavour to this fragrant zesty curd-based curry. If you can't manage to get your hands on it, you can easily substitute its media savy hipster cousin kaffir lime.

INGREDIENTS

1 kg chicken (with the bone)

1 cup curd

Salt to taste

2 tbsps ginger, juiced

2 tbsps garlic paste

½ cup onion, juiced

1 tsp Gondhoraj lemon juice

1 tbsp green chilli paste

½ tsp garam masala powder

1½ tsps coriander powder

½ tsp lemon zest

2 tbsps mustard oil

4 pods of green cardamom

1 inch-long cinnamon stick

6 tbsps onion paste, fine

4 green chillies, slit and de-seeded

½ tsp black pepper powder

1 Gondhoraj lebu or kaffir lime

7 Gondhoraj lebu leaves or kaffir lime leaves

1½ tsps sugar

Water as needed

METHOD

- Rinse the meat with cold water. Drain and set aside.
- Whip curd in a large bowl. Add a pinch of salt, ginger juice, garlic paste, onion juice, lime juice, green chilli paste, garam masala, coriander powder and lemon zest. Mix well.
- Add the chicken to this mix and marinate for 60-90 minutes.
- Heat oil in a saucepan. Splutter cardamom pods and add cinnamon.
- Sauté onion paste on low heat until it looks transparent.
- Add the marinated chicken and keep the excess marinade aside for later use. Cook with the lid on at medium low heat for about 10 minutes.
- Add the residual marination, some water, slit green chillies and black pepper powder. Mix well. Simmer with the lid on until the meat is cooked on medium low heat.
- Cut the lemon into several roundels. Add the roundels and the leaves along with the sugar to the saucepan.
- Turn off the heat and let it rest for 5 minutes.
- Serve with piping hot rice.

Goan Sausage Pulao

40 minutes | Serves  4-5

IN A NUTSHELL

From the land of susegad, Goan Sausage Pulao symbolises the Portuguese influence during colonisation. This hearty dish is meant for a languid lunch. It is made with an array of spices but derives it mainly from Chorice, a cured homemade sausage similar to a chorizo. Relish this spicy, tangy pulao with a pint of beer (or two!) and make the most of a laid back Sunday.

INGREDIENTS

- 2 ½ cups basmati rice (preferred, but can be substituted)
- 40 units of Goan rosary sausages (or 30 cocktail-sized sausages)
- 3 tbsps ghee (clarified butter)
- 2 bay leaves
- 9 of whole cloves
- 2 inch-long cinnamon stick
- 12 units of whole black peppercorns
- 2 units cardamom (optional or powdered is preferred)
- 1 tsp ginger-garlic paste
- 1 large onion finely chopped
- 1 medium-sized tomato, finely chopped
- ½ tsp turmeric powder
- 4 ¾ cups of water
- Salt to taste

METHOD

- Rinse the rice and drain. Keep aside.
- Release the sausage from the casing and chop coarsely.
- Place a saucepan on medium low heat and add ghee.
- Follow this by adding whole garam masala in the following order: bay leaves, cloves, cinnamon, black peppercorn and cardamom. Let it splutter.
- Once the splutter settles, add ginger-garlic paste followed by onion and fry until transparent.
- Add tomato and cook until the skin starts to separate from the flesh. Add turmeric and sauté for two more minutes. Stir continuously.
- Add the sausages and cook until the spices and lard mix well with the garam masala mix.
- Add rice and sauté for another 2 minutes. Add salt.
- Add water and let it simmer for about 5 minutes. Stir occasionally so the solids don't stick to the base of the pan.
- Cook until the water dries up, cover with a lid and let it sit for another 5 minutes. Serve hot!

THE
POT-SHOT!!

Gosht Ka Halwa

- ½ kg mutton, boneless and pulverised, preferably from the leg or shoulder of the lamb
- ½ litre water
- Salt to taste
- 1 pinch saffron
- 300 gm khoya (concentrated milk solids)
- 300 gm ghee (clarified butter)
- 1 tsp cardamom, powdered
- 60 ml rosewater
- 100 ml milk (optional)
- ½ kg sugar
- 50 gm almonds, soaked overnight and chopped
- 50 gm chironji (cudappah almonds)

IN A NUTSHELL

India is an ancient land that has over centuries witnessed civilisations, kingdoms, rulers, and governments. Over time, food has evolved too. Along with the evolution, there are some forgotten cuisines and recipes that lay on the sands of time like a shipwreck on a seabed. Gosht ka Halwa from the erstwhile Rampuri cuisine is one such delicacy deemed fit for a king.

METHOD

- Place the mutton in a bowl and rinse it twice with clean potable water
- Heat water in a pot, bring to a boil. Add a pinch of salt.
- Add the meat and let it boil for about 5 minutes or until tender.
- Drain and cool.
- In a bowl soak saffron in warm water.
- Add khoya to the meat and let it sit.
- In a separate pan, heat ghee and add the meat and khoya mix. Sauté until the meat starts to caramelise.
- Once it is a light shade of brown, add cardamom, rosewater, milk, and saffron. Stir well.
- Add sugar at regular intervals and keep stirring continuously until the mix amalgamates.
- Turn off the heat when the ingredients have come together. Add chopped almonds and chironji.
- Serve hot.

Gushtaba

Serves 5-6

IN A NUTSHELL

Gushtaba or Goshtaba is a meatball curry hailing from the northern most state in the country – Jammu & Kashmir. It is a part of the traditional Wazwan, this yoghurt based gravy is usually served in a formal banquet and the locals consider it fit for a royal feast.

INGREDIENTS

800 gm lamb, finely minced
1 tbsp cumin powder
200 gm meat fat
2 tbsps cardamom seeds
Salt to taste
1 egg white
6 tbsps mustard oil
1'x1' white muslin cloth
½ tsp dried ginger, powdered
21 inch-long cinnamon stick, powdered
2 ½ tbsps fennel powder
2 black cardamom, powdered
5 cloves, crushed
1 tbsp fenugreek seeds
1 tbsp coriander seeds, powdered
3 medium-sized onions, chopped
½ tbsp cumin seeds
1 ½ cups yoghurt, whipped
1 tbsp ghee (clarified butter)
1 litre water
2 bay leaves
A handful of coriander and mint leaves to garnish (optional)

METHOD

- Grind the mince and the fat until it becomes a luscious, smooth paste.
- In a bowl add minced lamb, cumin powder, cardamom seeds, salt, egg white and a tbsp of mustard oil. Mix evenly.
- Wash the muslin cloth clean of any dirt and starch, and dry.
- Add dried ginger powder, cinnamon, fennel powder, black cardamom powdered, cloves, fenugreek and powdered coriander seeds and tie it in the cloth. Ensure the knot is tight.
- In a huge pan, add a litre of water with bay leaves. Put in the spices tied in the muslin cloth. Bring to a boil on high flame.
- Divide the minced lamb into portions and roll them into 1 inch meatballs.
- As you roll these balls, put them into the boiling water and continue to boil on a low flame until the broth reduces to half.
- Remove the pouch of spices, give it a good squeeze and discard it.
- Remove the pan from the flame and set aside.
- In a separate pan, heat the rest of the oil and caramelise onions. Remove and grind coarsely.
- Splutter cumin seeds in the pan. Follow it by adding ground onions and yoghurt. Stir continuously so the yoghurt doesn't curdle.
- Add ghee, sauté for 30 seconds.
- Add the meatballs along with the broth and simmer for 5 minutes. Check for the salinity of the curry and adjust if required.
- Garnish with coriander and mint leaves. Serve with rice.

Indian Style Pork Chops

30 minutes | Serves 2

IN A NUTSHELL

Inspired by the spices found in a standard Indian kitchen, these pork chops are sweet, spicy and oh-so-delicious! This quick and easy recipe is a sure way to impress guests arriving on short notice. Cooked until tender, the meat slides off the bone and the lard seamlessly brings the flavours together.

INGREDIENTS

500 gms pork chops
½ tsp turmeric powder
Pepper to season
2 tbsps ghee (clarified butter)/unsalted butter
2 medium-sized onions, coarsely chopped
1 tsp ginger, minced
7 cloves of garlic, minced
1 tsp coriander powder
½ tbsp Kashmiri red chilli powder
½ tbsp garam masala
Salt to taste
2 medium-sized tomatoes, pureed
1 tbsp honey

METHOD

- Rinse and drain the meat. Pat dry with a paper towel.
- Sprinkle the meat with turmeric and pepper powders. Set aside.
- Heat 1 tbsp ghee in a skillet, add onions and caramelise.
- Add ginger, garlic, coriander, red chilli powder along with garam masala powder and sauté for 3 minutes. Season with salt.
- Add tomato puree and cook for another minute. Taste the sauce and add honey if required.
- In another skillet, add the rest of the ghee and shallow fry the chops until brown. Set aside.
- Add the chops to the tomato gravy mix. Mix well.
- Line a baking tray with foil coated with butter and preheat the oven to 180°C.
- Place the pork chops with the sauce on the baking tray and cook for 45 minutes.
- Serve hot!

THE POT-SHOT!!

Kasundi Tikka Bhel

40 minutes | Serves 6-8

IN A NUTSHELL

Bhel or jhalmuri is a well-revered street style snack. This recipe adds a kick of mustard with the use of kasundi marinated chicken. It makes for a delicious, healthy snack with protein and a robust mustard flavour.

INGREDIENTS

1 kg chicken fillets cut into cubes
3 tsps ginger-garlic paste
3 tsps garam masala
¼ cup hung curd
3 tbsps kasundi (mustard)
3 ½ tsps mustard oil
1 kg puffed rice
2 large tomatoes, finely chopped
3 large onions finely chopped
½ tsp red chilli powder
Salt to taste
½ cup raw mango, finely chopped
½ cup pomegranate
A pinch of chaat masala
1 tbsp lemon juice

METHOD

- Rinse the chicken cubes and place them in a large bowl.
- Marinade chicken with the ginger-garlic paste, garam masala powder, hung curd, kasundi mustard and 1 tbsp mustard oil for about 4 hours.
- Line a baking tray with aluminium foil or baking paper.
- Preheat the oven to 180 °C.
- Put the chicken cubes onto skewers and cook them until the chicken is well done.
- Remove from the oven and let it cool.
- In a large bowl, mix puffed rice, tomatoes, onions, red chilli powder, salt, and raw mango along with pomegranate.
- Pull apart the chicken tikka into shreds.
- Add the shredded chicken along with the residual marinade from the baking tray to the bowl of puffed rice and other ingredients.
- Ladle some into the dish. Sprinkle chaat masala, lemon juice and serve.

THE
POT-SHOT!!

Keema Samosas

Serves 

IN A NUTSHELL

Samosas are essentially deep-fried pockets of spiced filling, usually potato mash. Keema Samosas are a well-revered street style snack made with minced meat. They are best served hot on cold winter mornings with spicy green chilli chutney.

INGREDIENTS

2 cups of refined flour
¼ tsp carom seeds
Salt as required
1 ½ tbsps oil for kneading
Water as required
¼ kg minced meat
½ inch ginger
10 cloves of garlic
½ tsp cumin seeds
½ tsp black pepper powder
½ tsp cloves
1 brown cardamom
2 green cardamoms
Oil to deep fry
1 medium-sized onion, finely chopped
1 medium-sized tomato, deseeded and finely chopped
½ tsp garam masala
3 green chillies
1 tsp red chilli powder
¼ tsp turmeric powder
½ tsp coriander seeds, powdered

METHOD

- Use a sieve to sift the flour; add carom seeds, salt, some oil and water to knead stiff dough. Cover and set aside.
- Rinse the mince under running water using a strainer. Drain and squeeze any excess water.
- Grind ginger, garlic, cumin seeds, black pepper, cloves and cardamoms into a fine paste.
- Heat oil in a saucepan and fry onions until transparent. Add tomatoes along with the garam masala and cook with the lid on until the skin of the tomato starts peeling.
- Add chillies followed by the spice mix paste from the grinder.
- Add the minced meat, red chilli powder, turmeric powder, coriander powder and a cup of water. Cook with a lid on top for 10 minutes.
- Divide the dough into several spheres the size of a golf ball.
- Roll each ball into an oval and cut bilaterally. Then give the pastry a conical shape and stuff it with cooked mince.
- Seal the edges and cover with a moist muslin cloth. Let it sit for about 15 minutes.
- Heat oil for the deep fry and slide the samosas in gently. Once they are golden brown, take them out and dab with paper towel.
- Serve hot with sweet and sour tamarind chutney or fiery green chilli chutney.

THE
POT-SHOT!!

Kerala Style Duck Roast

 60 minutes | Serves 

IN A NUTSHELL

A popular Kerala dish, it hails from the Syrian Christian kitchens. This nostalgic dish is a staple on special occasions such as Christmas and Easter.

INGREDIENTS

Duck cut into 8-10 pieces, about 1.5 kgs

2 tbsps cooking oil

¼ kg onions

¼ kg shallots

2 tbsps ginger-garlic paste

A sprig of curry leaves

1 medium-sized tomato, julienned

2 tbsps red chilli powder

1 tbsp coriander powder

½ tsp turmeric powder

1 tsp fennel powder

1 tbsp garam masala

1 cup chicken stock

3 tbsps coconut milk

Salt to taste

Coriander leaves to garnish

METHOD

- In a deep saucepan, heat oil and sauté the onions along with the shallots until they start to caramelise.
- Add ginger-garlic paste and splutter curry leaves.
- Follow this by adding tomato along with chilli, coriander, turmeric, fennel, and garam masala powders. Sauté well until the spices come together.
- Add the duck and sauté for about a minute.
- Add stock/hot water and cook with the lid on for 20 minutes or until the water evaporates completely.
- Add the coconut milk and simmer for another 3-5 minutes. Season with salt after a taste test.
- Garnish with coriander leaves and serve hot with appam or rice.

My Desi Roast Chicken

Serves 4

IN A NUTSHELL

An ode to the classic roast chicken, My Desi Roast Chicken is an ode to the Indian spices and condiments. Meant to be shared with friends and family, it is ideal for a Sunday lunch; it has the power to summon the strongest of hunger pangs before you relish it and to lull you into a food coma afterward!

INGREDIENTS

One whole chicken, skin on, 1.5-1.75kgs

3 tbsps Kashmiri red chilli powder

2 tbsps ginger paste

1 tbsp garlic paste

½ tbsp pepper powder

1 tsp cumin powder

1 tbsp honey

1 ½ tbsp vinegar

1 tsp garam masala powder

1/4 cup butter, melted

Salt to taste

3 potatoes, cut into four parts

3 onions, cut into four parts

3 pods garlic (whole, halved)

1 lemon (sliced)

METHOD

- Wash the chicken and pat dry.
- In a large mixing bowl, add chilli powder, ginger, garlic paste, pepper powder, cumin powder, honey, vinegar, garam masala powder, butter and salt into a smooth paste.
- Apply the chilli paste all over the chicken; ensure that it's spread evenly covering all the chicken into the crevices and under the skin. Reserve the extra marinade for later. If you have extra marinade remaining, you can use it to brush the chicken while it cooks.
- Cover and let it marinate for at least 2 hours, ideally overnight in the refrigerator.
- If you leave it in the fridge, remove it 45 minutes before cooking to let it reach room temperature.
- Use an oven proof baking dish and add potatoes, onions, garlic and lemon slices to the bottom.
- Tie the chicken legs together with a kitchen string and transfer it on top of the veggies.

- Bake in a pre-heated oven at 220°C for 90 minutes. Keep brushing the chicken with the fats and gravy from the pan every 30 minutes or so.
- Just about 5 minutes before the chicken cooks entirely, brush it with the marinade one final time in the last 5 minutes.
- Once cooked, let it rest for 10-15 minutes.
- Serve hot with roti or bread with a salad of your choice.

Mutton Dhansak

 90 minutes | Serves  6-8

INGREDIENTS

1 kg boneless mutton, chopped into 1 inch cubes

2 tbsps *masoor daal* (red split lentils)

2 tbsps *toor daal* (split pigeon peas)

1 ½ tsps ginger-garlic paste

Salt to taste

½ cup oil

¼ tsp black cumin seeds

2 medium-sized onions, julienned

½ tsp fenugreek seeds or leaves, finely chopped

1 cup aubergine, chopped

½ cup pumpkin, chopped

1 potato, chopped

2 medium-sized tomatoes, chopped

½ cup carrots, chopped

½ cup spinach, chopped

2-3 green chillies, chopped

A pinch of turmeric powder

1 tsp coriander powder

1 tsp red chilli powder

1 tsp cumin powder

1 tsp dhansak garam masala

1 ½ cup mutton stock (optional)

5 cups water

METHOD

- In a vessel, add all the lentils and rinse. Soak for either overnight or minimum 4-6 hours.
- Marinate meat with a tsp of ginger-garlic paste and salt either overnight or minimum 4-6 hours.
- In a pressure cooker or a heavy bottomed pan, heat ¼ cup oil. Temper with black cumin seeds.
- Add the rest of the ginger-garlic paste and onion. Sauté until the onions are transparent.
- Add fenugreek seeds (or leaves) along with aubergine, pumpkin, potato, tomatoes, carrots, and spinach.
- Follow this with green chillies, turmeric powder, coriander powder, red chilli powder, cumin powder and dhansak garam masala. Sauté until all the vegetables are slightly cooked and coated with masala
- Add the soaked lentils and 3 cups of water. Cover with a lid and let it cook. If you're using a pressure cooker, cook for about 3 whistles or 10 minutes.
- In a separate Crockpot, heat rest of the oil and add the marinated meat.
- Sauté for 30 seconds and add mutton stock. Cook for about 10 minutes, until the meat is semi-cooked.

IN A NUTSHELL

Arguably one of the most popular Parsi delicacies, this meat and lentil curry sees an amalgam of Persian and Gujarati cuisines. This curry is time consuming and hence reserved for Sundays for a languid lunch that is followed by a lazy siesta.

- Once the lentils and vegetable mix is cooked and cooled, use a hand blender to blend until it reaches a thick consistency.
- Add this mix to the mutton and simmer for another 10 minutes. You can use mutton stock or water if it becomes too thick.
- Once cooked, serve with rice and a wedge of lime.

Mutton Sambar

30 minutes | Serves 4

INGREDIENTS

½ kg mutton, curry cut
Salt to taste
1 cup *toor dal* (split pigeon peas)
1 large tomato, blanched and coarsely chopped
2 tsp coriander leaves
1 tsp sambar masala powder
2 tbsps coconut, freshly grated
1 tbsp oil
1 large onion, finely copped
3 cloves of garlic, finely chopped
1 inch ginger
½ tsp turmeric powder
2 cups mutton stock

THE POT-SHOT!!

IN A NUTSHELL

Hailing from the Coromandel Coast, Mutton Sambar draws its origins from many colonies the coast has stood witness to. This comforting lentil curry, unlike the popular version, has chunks of lamb and is best savoured with piping hot steamed rice and pickle.

METHOD

- Rinse and drain the mutton under cold water. Rub in some salt and keep aside.
- Rinse and soak lentils for 30 minutes. Drain and set aside.
- Grind tomato, coriander leaves and sambar powder into a fine paste.
- Grind the coconut into a fine paste in a separate container and keep aside.
- Heat oil in a pressure cooker or a heavy bottom saucepan; sauté onions until transparent.
- Add garlic and ginger. Fry until it starts to caramelise.
- Add turmeric powder followed by lentils (split pigeon peas) and ground tomato paste. Mix well.
- Add mutton and coconut paste. Cook for 4-5 minutes, stirring continuously.
- Add the mutton stock and cook with the lid on for 15-20 minutes until the meat is cooked.
- Serve hot with rice.

North Eastern Jadoh Rice

60-70 minutes | Serves 6-8

IN A NUTSHELL

Literally translating to meat and rice, Jadoh is a delicacy of the Khasi tribe in Meghalaya. Simple, delicious and easy to make, it is ideal for a quick lunch, especially when you look forward to a busy day or a night in.

INGREDIENTS

1 cup pork belly, cut into cubes

2 cups of joha rice (substitute with any other short grain rice)

2 tbsps oil

1 medium-sized onion, finely chopped

1 tbsp ginger paste

½ tsp of turmeric

1 tsp black pepper, powdered

2 bay leaves

Salt to taste

4 cups water

Fresh coriander to garnish

METHOD

- Cut the pork into ½ inch cubes and rinse with cold water. Set aside.
- Wash and drain the rice. Keep aside.
- Heat oil in a saucepan. Add onions, ginger paste, turmeric and black pepper.
- Sauté the ingredients until the onions are transparent and the ingredients mix well.
- Use a flame gun to burn the tip of the bay leaves and place them into the pan.
- Add the pork and sear until it turns golden brown and the lard melts.
- Add washed rice to the pan. Sauté for 2-3 minutes until the rice, meat and spices mix properly. Add salt.
- Add water and cook with the lid on. Simmer until the water evaporates and the rice and meat are cooked well.
- Garnish with coriander and serve hot.

Pork Belly Roast

60 minutes | Serves 

IN A NUTSHELL

Who doesn't like pork belly? A quick and minimal recipe, the crispy skin and luscious soft spiced belly make for a good meal served with bread or naan with perhaps salad of your choice.

INGREDIENTS

750 gms pork belly scored

4 tsps whole peppercorns

4 tsps cumin seeds

1 tsp methi seeds (fenugreek)

1 inch-long cinnamon stick

3 tbsps coriander seeds

1 tsp mustard seeds

2 tsps red chilli powder

1 tsp turmeric powder

2 tsps garlic powder

1 tsp sugar

3 tbsps water

½ tbsp salt

METHOD

- Dry roast all the spices (i.e. whole peppercorns, cumin seeds, fenugreek seeds, cinnamon, coriander seeds, mustard seeds) for about 10 minutes.
- Let it cool, then add to a grinder along with red chilli powder, turmeric powder and garlic powder. Grind in to a coarse paste. Add sugar and water to adjust the consistency.
- In a large mixing bowl, add the pork belly and spice paste. Rub it in well and let it marinate, and then add salt. Preheat the oven to 180°C.
- Place the belly on a roasting tray and cook for 45 minutes. Check occasionally.
- Increase the temperature to 220°C and cook for 10 minutes or until the skin is crispy. Rest the belly until needed.
- In the meanwhile, scrape the residual drippings from the roasting tray. Transfer

Railway Mutton Curry

50 minutes | Serves  5-6

METHOD

- Rinse and drain the mutton under cold water.
- In a large mixing bowl, add curd, ginger-garlic paste, turmeric powder, mustard oil, Kashmiri red chilli powder and salt. Marinate overnight or at least for 180 minutes.
- Dry roast fennel seeds, black peppercorn, coriander and cumin seeds for up to 5 minutes, stirring occasionally, and grind into a fine powder.
- Shallow fry the potatoes in a pan until they turn golden brown and keep aside.

INGREDIENTS

FOR THE GRAVY:

2 medium-sized potatoes, cut into halves

4 tbsps mustard oil

1 bay leaf

1 mace

1 black cardamom, whole

2 green cardamom pods

½ inch-long cinnamon stick

2 whole cloves

1 tsp ginger-garlic paste

1 medium-sized onion, julienned

2 green chillies, slit vertically

½ tsp turmeric powder

1 tsp Kashmiri red chilli powder

2 medium-sized tomatoes, pureed

2 cups chicken stock

1 tsp ghee (clarified butter)

½ tsp garam masala powder

IN A NUTSHELL

A culinary trip to zcolonial times, this curry was a mellowed variant of the spicy Indian curry adapted for the British officers' palate stationed in Kolkata. This delicately spiced curry brings out all the flavours of the eclectic spices used. Serve and relish with luchi, rice or even roti, and lull yourself into a food coma.

FOR MARINATION:

mutton with bone, 750 gms

1 tbsp curd or lemon juice

1 tsp ginger-garlic paste

½ tsp turmeric powder

1 tsp mustard oil

½ tsp Kashmiri red chilli powder

Salt to taste

FOR DRY ROASTING:

½ fennel seeds

5 black peppercorns, whole

½ tsp coriander seeds

½ tsp cumin seeds

- In a large saucepan heat some oil and bring it to its smoking point.
- Add the whole garam masala (i.e. bay leaf, mace, black and green cardamoms, cinnamon and cloves) and fry until the flavour infuses in the warm oil.
- Add ginger-garlic paste and sauté for about 3-5 minutes. Add onion and fry until it starts to caramelise.
- Follow this with green chillies, turmeric powder and Kashmiri red chilli powder along with the dry roasted powder. Sauté for another 5 minutes.
- Turn up the heat to medium high and add the marinated mutton pieces. Stir continuously.
- Add the tomato puree and fried potatoes. Mix well.
- Add the chicken stock simmer until the curry reaches the desired consistency and the meat cooks.
- Add a spoonful of ghee and ½ tsp garam masala. Cook further for 2-5 minutes.
- Turn off the heat and let it sit 10 minutes.
- Serve hot with hot puffed luchi, rice or even roti.

Mangalorean Sukka Chicken

30-35 minutes | Serves 2

INGREDIENTS

½ kg chicken, preferably boneless

1 tsp red chilli powder

1 tsp black pepper powder

½ tsp fennel powder

2 tsps coriander powder

Salt to taste

2 tbsps yoghurt

2 tbsps oil (or ghee)

¾ tbsp ginger-garlic paste

1 medium-sized onion (or 10 shallots), finely chopped

½ tsp garam masala powder

¼ tsp turmeric powder

2 green chillies, slit

A handful of coriander leaves, chopped (optional)

IN A NUTSHELL

Hailing from the western coastal state of Karnataka, Mangalorean Sukka Chicken is a fiery local dish that doubles up as a snack, side or an appetiser. Locals and natives consider this to be a bar grub that pairs well with a chilled pint of beer.

METHOD

- Cut the chicken into cubes and rinse with cold water. Transfer to a mixing bowl.
- Add the red chilli powder, black pepper powder, fennel powder, coriander powder and salt to the mixing bowl.
- Follow this with yoghurt, mix well and coat the chicken with it. Let this mix marinade for at least 30 minutes.
- In a saucepan or wok, heat oil on a medium high flame.
- Splutter ginger-garlic paste, follow this by adding onion and fry until golden brown.
- Add garam masala powder and turmeric powder. Sauté for a minute until the spices mix properly. Stir continuously.
- Add the slit green chillies, cover and cook for 3 more minutes.
- Add the marinated chicken to this pan. Sauté for 4 minutes, stir occasionally.
- Add some warm water and put the lid on to cook until the water evaporates and the meat is thoroughly cooked.
- Garnish with chopped coriander leaves. Serve hot with flatbreads, rice or savour just as is.

A part of Wazwan, the highest form of a Kashmiri Muslim banquet, Lahabi Kebab is a comforting dish that comes with its own curries. These meticulously crafted kebabs in tomato-based gravy seem to be perfect for a languid meal relished with roti, bread or rice.

INGREDIENTS

½ kg mutton, minced

1 medium-sized onion, finely chopped

1 egg

3 tsps Kashmiri red chilli powder

1 tsp garam masala powder

2 pods of cardamom, crushed

Salt to taste

1 ½ tsp ginger-garlic paste

5 mint leaves

Oil as needed

½ tsp coriander powder

- Mix well using your hands or a spatula. If the consistency seems coarse, grind it into a paste.
- Add chopped mint leaves along with the residual onion and shape into a sphere. Flatten into cutlets.
- Heat oil in a skillet and fry kebabs until brown.
- Pat with a paper towel and set aside.
- Add tomato puree, onion, red chillies and coriander powder in a grinder and make a thick, dense paste.
- Heat oil in a saucepan; splutter and sauté ginger-garlic paste for 2 minutes.
- Add the tomato puree paste and sauté for 3 minutes.
- Follow this by adding curd, turmeric powder, cardamoms and coriander powder. Cook for 3-4 more minutes.
- Once the curry starts to cook, add chicken stock for desired consistency and bring to a boil.
- Reduce the heat and let it simmer till it reaches the consistency required. Check for the salinity and adjust as per your taste.
- Turn off the heat and add the kebabs. Let them sit for about 5 minutes and serve hot with rotis, bread or rice.

FOR CURRY:

½ kg tomato puree

1 medium-sized onion

4 red chillies

½ tsp coriander powder

½ cup oil

1 tsp ginger-garlic paste

½ cup curd

1 tsp turmeric powder

2 pods cardamoms

1 cup chicken stock

Tujji Kebab

Serves 

IN A NUTSHELL

Comprising a course of the Kashmiri Wazwan, Tujji Kebab is a quick fix appetiser that is also ideal for serving as finger food on a night when hosting friends or a night spent indoors.

INGREDIENTS

1 kg chicken, boneless
2 tsps ginger paste
2 tsps garlic paste
2 tsps cumin powder
2 tsps garam masala powder
3 tsps red chilli powder
Salt to taste
2 tsps lemon juice
1 tsp turmeric powder
1 tbsp mustard oil

METHOD

- Dice the chicken and rinse in cold water. Transfer to a large mixing bowl.
- Add ginger and garlic pastes, cumin powder, garam masala powder, red chilli powder, salt, lemon juice and turmeric powder. Cover with a cling film and set aside to marinade for 2 hours.
- Remove any excess juices or water from the chicken and preheat oven to 180°C.

- Coat the baking tray with mustard oil and put chicken into skewers.
- Mix the residual mustard oil and the juices from the marinade and baste the chicken with this.
- Place it on the baking tray and set in the oven for 5-10 minutes until it cooks.
- Serve hot with mint chutney, lime wedges and onion.

Saoji Mutton

INGREDIENTS

1 kg mutton cut into pieces on the bone, or lamb shanks

5 tbsps cooking oil

2 tbsps coriander seeds

1 tsp cumin seeds

1 tbsp ginger, finely chopped

8 cloves of garlic

2 pods of black cardamoms

1 pod of green cardamom

6 dried red chillies

6 cloves

1 tbsp black peppercorns

1 ½ inch-long cinnamon stick

1 bay leaf

1 tsp poppy seeds

1 tbsp stone flower

½ cup dried coconut flakes

4 medium-sized onions, julienned

2 tbsps sorghum flour

½ kg mutton, curry cut

½ tsp turmeric powder

Salt to taste

1 ½ tbsps Kashmiri red chilli powder

2 cups mutton stock

IN A NUTSHELL

Saoji or Savji is a lesser known central Maharashtrian tribe and Saoji Mutton is arguably the most popular delicacy from the eponymous cuisine. Unlike most of the other curries in the region, this one gets its spice quotient from the use of black pepper and a mix of dry roasted spices. It isn't uncommon to see the people huddled around the table at home and local street vendors savouring this fiery curry when the mercury drops and there's a nip in the air. Served with a side of bhakri or rice, it warms you up on a cold night and puts you to sleep too.

METHOD

- Heat 1 tbsp oil in a pan. Splutter coriander seeds and cumin seeds.
- Add ginger and garlic; sauté for a minute.
- Add black and green cardamoms, dried red chillies, cloves, black peppercorn, cinnamon, bay leaf, poppy seeds, stone flower and dried coconut. Sauté till the fragrance of the spices wafts.
- Add onions and fry until they start to caramelise. Follow this with sorghum flour and sauté for a minute.
- Cool the spice mix and grind into a fine, smooth paste. Add water if required.
- In a pressure cooker, heat a tbsp of oil and add mutton. Sauté for a minute or two.
- Add turmeric powder and salt, stir well. Cook with the lid on for 6-7 whistles.
- In another saucepan heat 2 tbsps of oil and sauté the spice paste. Add red chilli powder and mix well.
- Add the cooked mutton to the saucepan, mix well and add the mutton stock to adjust the volume of the gravy until it reaches the desired consistency.
- Simmer until the mutton is cooked and the gravy has reached the desired consistency.
- Serve hot with bhakri or rice.

Thecha Chicken Kebabs

30 minutes | Serves 3-4

IN A NUTSHELL

Inspired by the dip from central Maharashtra, Thecha isn't for the weak hearted. Chicken kebabs marinated in fiery green chilli spice mix and grilled lend it a smoky delicious flavour. Relished as an appetiser or a snack, Thecha Chicken Kebabs pair well with most pilsners, lagers and India Pale Ales (IPAs).

5 chicken breasts, boneless
12 bamboo skewers
15-18 green chillies, deseeded
10-12 cloves of garlic, crushed
1 tsp cumin powder
A handful of coriander leaves
3 tsps lime juice
Salt to taste
½ tsp asafoetida

METHOD

- Cut the chicken breast in long strips.
- Soak bamboo skewers in cold water.
- Grind chillies, garlic, cumin powder, coriander leaves, lime juice, salt, and asafoetida into a coarse, dense paste.
- Tenderise the meat slightly using a tenderiser. Put the skewers through the chicken.
- Marinate the chicken in skewers with the ground paste for at least 60 minutes.
- Preheat the oven to 180°C. Line a baking tray with greased foil and place the skewers on it for about 15 minutes or a barbeque until the meat is slightly charred and cooked.
- Serve hot with curd, mayonnaise or ranch.

Sindhi Teevan Mutton Curry

60 minutes | Serves 3

curry with tenderly cooked mutton on the bone, this recipe is indigenous to the Sindhi community. It is traditionally known as Teevan within the Sindhi community. Usually eaten with rice or rotis, this delicious curry also pairs well with puris.

INGREDIENTS

½ kg mutton, curry cut

3 tbsps cooking oil

1 bay leaf

1 pod of black cardamom

½ inch-long cinnamon stick

2 large onions, finely chopped

1 tbsp ginger-garlic paste

½ tsp turmeric powder

4 green chillies, finely chopped

Salt to taste

1 tsp red chilli powder

1 small tomato, finely chopped and pureed

2 tsps coriander powder

1 tbsp curd, beaten to supple consistency

2 cups mutton stock

1 tsp garam masala powder

METHOD

- Heat oil in a saucepan. Sauté bay leaf, cardamom and cinnamon.
- Add the onions and sauté till they turn transparent.
- Add ginger-garlic paste, turmeric powder, green chillies and salt.
- Add the mutton and sauté for about 5 minutes or until the mutton starts to caramelise, stirring occasionally.
- Add the red chilli powder, tomato puree coriander powder and curd. Sauté well.
- Use the mutton stock to adjust the consistency of the curry and bring to a boil on medium high heat.
- Reduce the heat and add garam masala powder. Cook for an hour or until the meat is tender.
- Serve hot with rotis or rice.

Bhujing

60-70 minutes | Serves  6-8

IN A NUTSHELL

Arguably Mumbai's oldest original street food, Bhujing is a feisty snack. Conceived on the periphery of the city, Agashi Bhujing Centre in Virar is believed to be the first place to serve it. A popular breakfast favourite of the locals it isn't unsurprising to see this tiny eatery teeming with both locals and the people summoned from far away.

INGREDIENTS

1 kg chicken, cut into cubes
5 medium-sized potatoes
Salt to taste
1 tsp cumin powder
½ tsp turmeric powder
1 bowl grated dry coconut
1 bowl of coriander leaves and green chillies paste
2 tsps garam masala powder
2 tbsp canola oil
4 medium-sized onions, julienned
2 tsps ginger-garlic paste
400 gm flattened rice

METHOD

- In a mixing bowl, add potatoes, chicken, salt, and cumin and turmeric powder. Set aside for about 30-60 minutes.
- Soak skewers in cold water take them out, dab with a towel.
- Preheat the oven to 180°C.
- Skewer the chicken and potatoes and roast for 5-8 minutes.
- Grind the coconut, green chillies, coriander leaves and garam masala into a fine paste.
- Heat oil in a pan and sauté julienned onions on a medium flame.
- Add the ginger-garlic paste followed by the spice paste to the pan and sauté for a couple of minutes.
- Add the chicken and potatoes mixture and cook well.
- Add flattened rice and mix well. Serve hot.

Chicken Soola Kebab

INGREDIENTS

6 chicken breasts

1 tbsp cloves

6 green cardamom seeds

2 tbsps black pepper

1 tbsp fennel seeds

1 tbsp cumin seeds

½ tbsp coriander seeds

2 tbsps mustard oil

3 tbsps ghee

1 medium-sized onion, finely chopped

8 garlic cloves, finely chopped

1 cup coriander leaves

Salt to taste

½ cup plain curd

Bamboo skewers as needed

Chaat masala to sprinkle

2 lemons, juiced

IN A NUTSHELL

Hailing from the north western state of Rajasthan, Soola is a spice mix made using earthy spices. We've used chicken but this ensemble of spices is versatile enough to work with red meat and seafood too. Make these delicious kebabs before a game night or for a dinner party, if you have any left over you could probably make a roll or sandwich out of it too!

METHOD

- In a skillet dry roast cloves, cardamom, black pepper, fennel, cumin, coriander seeds.
- Allow this mix to cool and grind them into a fine powder. Set aside.
- In a pan heat oil and ghee together on low heat to ensure it doesn't burn. Add onion and sauté until it is transparent.
- Add garlic and sauté for one more minute. Transfer to a plate and allow it to cool.
- Grind onion-garlic mix, ground spices and coriander leaves along with a pinch of salt into a smooth paste.
- Once done, add this to the curd and whisk well.
- Cut the chicken pieces into cubes and add it to the bowl of curd. Mix well to ensure the chicken is coated on all sides. Cover with cling film and set aside to marinade for at least 4 hours.
- Soak the bamboo skewers in water for about 15 minutes. Remove and pat dry.
- Once the chicken is back to room temperature, put it onto the skewers and grill over an open flame.
- Keep turning the skewers as needed to ensure the chicken is evenly cooked while slightly charred on the outside for the smoky flavour.
- Transfer to a plate, sprinkle with chaat masala and lemon juice.
- Serve hot with salad, raita, or the mint-green chilli chutney.

Sister-In-Law's Brain Pakora

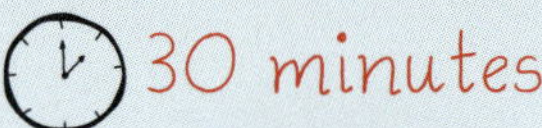

3-4 goat brains
2-3 cups water
Salt as needed
¼ turmeric powder
2 whole cardamoms
1 small piece cinnamon
2-3 cloves
¼ tsp saunf/aniseeds
¼ tsp cumin powder
Red chilli powder as needed
¼ tsp garam masala powder
1 cup besan/chick pea flour
A pinch of baking soda
Oil to fry

IN A NUTSHELL

Delicious Brain Pakora straight from my sister-in-law's kitchen is cooked in pickling spices. This hearty and wholesome dish can be relished as a side or by itself.

METHOD

- Immerse the brains in water and clean them carefully. Remove the top skin and veins.
- In a pan, take 2-3 cups water and boil the brains. Add salt, turmeric powder, cardamoms, cinnamon, cloves and aniseeds.
- Turn the side once and boil until done (4-5 minutes). Remove and set aside to cool.
- Cut them into big pieces (chunks). Sprinkle cumin powder, red chilli powder and garam masala on them.
- Make the batter with besan, salt, baking soda and water as required.
- Heat oil in a frying pan. Dip the brains in the batter and fry until golden brown and crispy.
- Serve hot.

Shab Daig

60 minutes | Serves 4

IN A NUTSHELL

Native to the beautiful valley of Kashmir, Shab Daig literally translates to night cauldron. A well-revered broth, it is usually slow cooked in winters for dinner. This turnip and meat gravy can be made with beef, chicken or lamb, and relished with either flatbreads or rice.

INGREDIENTS

½ cup ghee
1 medium-sized onion, sliced
6 medium-sized turnips, peeled
2 tsps ginger-garlic paste
1 tsp fennel seeds
1 inch-long cinnamon stick
4 cloves
2 tsps red chilli powder
1 cup yoghurt
½ kg lamb

FOR MEATBALLS:

½ kg lamb, minced
2 tsps ginger-garlic paste
1 tsp dried ginger powder
1 tsp Kashmiri or red chillies powder
¼ cup coriander leaves, chopped
1 green chilli, finely chopped
2 tbsps gram flour
1 egg
2 cups mutton stock

METHOD

- Heat ghee in a saucepan and fry onions until golden brown. Set aside.
- Fry turnips until golden brown in the same ghee. Remove and set aside.
- Add ginger-garlic paste, fennel seeds, cinnamon, cloves and red chilli powder to the skillet. Sauté for about a minute or until the spices come together in the pan.
- Cool and grind into a fine paste along with yoghurt.
- In the same pan, add turnips and lamb and fry until golden.
- Add masala paste and sauté till it separates.
- Add mutton stock and cook with the lid on top until the lamb cooks.
- Add all the ingredients listed under the meatball list in a grinder. Make a smooth paste.
- Mould into bite-sized balls and add them to the simmering pot.
- Add some more chicken stock if required. Cook until the meat tenderises and stir occasionally.
- Serve hot with steamed rice.

Salli Par Eedu

 15 minutes | Serves 

IN A NUTSHELL

Potatoes and eggs? Did someone say breakfast? This quick fix dish is a Parsi breakfast favourite. Easily described as a sunny side up on a bed of potato strings, Salli Par Eedu is replete with energy making it a great dish to start your day!

INGREDIENTS

2 tbsps oil

2 green chillies, finely chopped

1 cup coriander leaves, finely chopped

1 medium-sized tomato, finely chopped

1 tbsp ginger-garlic paste

1 tsp turmeric powder

2 tsps red chilli powder

1 tsp garam masala

Salt to taste

¼ kg fine potato strings

2 eggs

METHOD

- Heat oil in a deep skillet and add green chillies, coriander leaves and tomato. Sauté for 2 minutes.
- Add the ginger-garlic paste followed by turmeric powder, red chilli powder and garam masala. Sauté until all the ingredients merge and add salt.
- Add the thin potato strings and spread the mix across the pan evenly.
- Break the eggs and pour on to the potato strings. Sprinkle some water if required and cover to let it cook for another 5 minutes or until the eggs are firm but the yolk is slightly runny.
- Turn over to cook on the other side for another 2 minutes.
- Take it off the heat.
- Serve hot with buttered buns.

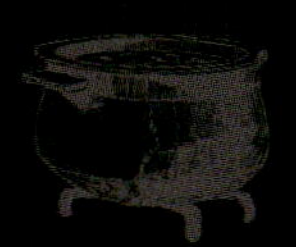

Ros Omelette

 40 minutes | Serves 

INGREDIENTS

2 tbsps oil

1 medium-sized onion, finely chopped

Salt to taste

1 tsp ginger-garlic paste

½ tsp turmeric powder

½ red chilli powder

1 large tomato, finely chopped

¼ tsp garam masala powder

1 tsp green chillies, finely chopped

2 tbsps fresh coconut, scraped and ground

2 eggs

1 tsp mint leaves, chopped

¼ tsp pepper powder

1 tsp coriander leaves, chopped

IN A NUTSHELL

Hailing from the coastal state of Goa, Ros Omelette or Ras Omelette is a street style snack. It's not unusual to spot local vendors selling this by the street, especially in tourist hubs. This Goan dish comprises of an omelette doused in robust gravy with a coconut base. Ros Omelette makes for a scrumptious snack or a mini-meal.

METHOD

- Heat oil in a pan; add chopped onion and a pinch of salt. Sauté until transparent.
- Add ginger-garlic paste, turmeric and red chilli powder and tomato. Cover it with a lid and cook for about 2-3 minutes.
- Remove the lid and add garam masala powder and green chillies. Sauté for about 30 seconds.
- Add ground coconut paste and cook for about 3 more minutes. If the mixture is a little thick, add some water and let it cook.
- In the meanwhile, beat eggs in a bowl and add mint, pepper powder, coriander leaves and salt to taste.
- In a separate pan, make an omelette.
- To serve, place the omelette in a bowl and ladle the gravy over. Serve with pao, roti, or sliced bread.

Rista Curry

Serves

IN A NUTSHELL

One of the lesser known culinary gems from the northern state of Kashmir, Rista is a simple yet delicious meatball curry. It is a part of the traditional Wazwan. Ideal for cold winter nights, relish it with rice, roti, naan or bread.

INGREDIENTS

FOR THE MEATBALLS:

¾ kg mutton, finely ground

2 tbsps mustard oil

7 pods of garlic, finely grated

1 tsp ginger powder

1 tsp fennel powder

Salt to taste

FOR THE GRAVY:

2 tbsps mustard oil

1 medium-sized onion, finely chopped

1 tsp cumin seeds

½ tsp asafoetida

1 tbsp Kashmiri red chilli powder

1 ½ tsps ginger, ground into fine paste

1 tsp fennel powder

2 pods of black cardamoms, crushed

1 tsp saffron threads

2 cups mutton stock

1 tbsp coriander leaves, chopped (optional)

Salt to taste

METHOD

- In a mixing bowl, add the mutton, mustard oil, garlic, ginger and fennel powders, and season with salt.
- Shape into 1 inch balls and cover with cling film. Set aside for 4 hours.
- Heat oil in a saucepan; add onion and sauté until transparent.
- Splutter cumin seeds followed by asafoetida. Add red chilli powder, ground ginger, fennel powder, black cardamom pods, and saffron threads. Sauté until the spices mix uniformly.
- Add mutton stock to the pan, bring to a boil. Lower the heat and simmer for about 5 minutes.
- Add the meatballs and cook with the lid on until meat cooks, approximately 30 minutes. Check on the consistency and add more stock if needed to get to the desired consistency.
- Garnish with coriander leaves and serve hot with bread, roti or rice.

THE POT-SHOT!!

Rajasthani Style Keema

INGREDIENTS

1 kg mutton, minced

1 tsp cumin seeds

2 inch-long cinnamon stick

¼ tsp cloves

½ tsp black peppercorns, whole

3 cardamoms

3 tbsps papaya, raw

1 tsp red chilli powder

2 tsps cumin powder

2 tsps red chillies, crushed

1 tbsp coriander powder

4 tbsps desiccated coconut

1 cup yoghurt

1 tbsp cooking oil

4 medium-sized onions, sliced

1 tbsp ginger-garlic paste

METHOD

- Dry roast cumin seeds, cinnamon, cloves, black peppercorns and cardamoms.
- Cool and grind them into a fine powder. Set aside.
- Put in papaya and grind into a fine thick paste using water to adjust consistency.
- In a large mixing bowl, add minced meat, dry spice powder set aside earlier and red chilli powder, cumin powder, crushed red chillies, coriander powder, papaya paste, desiccated coconut and yoghurt. Mix well.
- Cover this with cling film and leave to marinade for a maximum period of 5 hours.
- Heat oil in a pan, add onions and sauté until they start to caramelise.
- Add ginger-garlic paste and sauté for another minute.
- Follow this by adding the marinated mince.
- Slow cook on low flame with the lid on top until the meat tenderises. Stir occasionally to ensure it doesn't stick to the bottom of the pan.
- Once the meat is cooked, take off the heat.
- Serve hot with your choice of bread and a crisp salad.

IN A NUTSHELL

Easy to make and delicious to eat, this Rajasthani inspired minced meat dish uses papaya to tenderise the meat, lending it a peculiar taste and consistency. You can savour it with bread or roti. If you want other ways to savour it, you can place it in a canapé and garnish with a slit green chili or make it into a paratha.

Mirchi Malai Quail

40 minutes | Serves 3

IN A NUTSHELL

Fiery and delicious, Mirchi Malai Quail is inspired by a Rajasthani curry of the same name. It uses cream and chillies that bring out the distinct flavour, both contrasting and complimenting each other. Relished best with roti, bread or rice, it is ideal for cool winter nights.

INGREDIENTS

- ½ kg quail
- 3 tbsp cream
- ½ cup curd
- 5 green chillies, deseeded and finely chopped
- 1 medium-sized onion, finely chopped
- 1 tsp ginger paste
- 1 tsp garlic paste
- Water as needed
- Salt to taste
- 1 tsp black pepper powder
- 3 tbsp cooking oil
- 2 pods of green cardamom
- 5 black peppercorns
- 4 cloves
- 2 bay leaves
- 1 tsp garam masala powder
- ½ tbsp cashew paste
- 1 tsp kasuri methi
- ½ tsp sugar
- 2 tsp ghee

METHOD

- Clean the quail under running water.
- Whisk cream and curd together. Set aside in a cool place for further use.
- Grind green chillies, onion, ginger and garlic into a fine paste. Use water to adjust the consistency.
- Transfer to a large mixing bowl. Add salt and pepper, cover with a cling film and set aside for 60 minutes.
- Heat oil a wok or a saucepan and add the whole garam masala i.e. green cardamom, black peppercorns, cloves and bay leaves. Sauté until the aroma wafts.
- Add the spice paste to the pan followed by garam masala powder and sauté until the oil starts to separate.
- Add the cashew paste and stir continuously until it cooks for about 1 minute.
- Add the minimally marinated quail and let it cook until the meat starts to brown on the edges.
- Add curd, kasuri methi and sauté for a minute. Add water to get the desired consistency. Bring to a boil and simmer on medium low heat with the lid on for 10 minutes. Add sugar and ghee. Cook for 5 more minutes.
- Serve hot with bread, roti, or rice and a salad of your choice.

Kofte Ka Shorba

(Meatballs in Roasted Tomato Garlic Soup)

 70 minutes | Serves  5-6

IN A NUTSHELL

Sourced from a secret family recipe book, this broth comforts you on a cold night or after a long day. A fairly standard recipe, this can double as a meal if you add noodles to it.

INGREDIENTS

3 tbsps olive oil

1 kg tomatoes, cut into halves

8 garlic cloves, peeled

Salt and pepper to season

2 onions, julienned

1 cup vegetable stock

2 bay leaves

FOR THE MEATBALLS:

400g minced meat

2 garlic cloves

¼ cup basil leaves

1 tsp cumin powder

1 tsp coriander powder

1 tsp fennel powder

METHOD

- Preheat the oven to 200°C.
- Coat the baking tray with olive oil and place the tomatoes and garlic. Season with salt and pepper.
- Place the baking tray in the oven and roast the tomatoes and garlic for 30 minutes.
- Heat olive oil in a skillet and add onions. Sauté and caramelise the onions.
- Remove from heat and keep aside.
- Grind the minced meat, garlic, basil leaves, cumin, coriander and fennel powders into a fine paste. Cover with a cling film and set aside for 15 minutes.
- Grind the roasted tomatoes and garlic into a dense puree.
- Heat the vegetable stock in a pot and add bay leaves. Bring to a boil and simmer for a minute.
- Remove the bay leaves and add tomato-garlic puree.
- Use an immersion blender to blend into a runny broth and bring to a boil.
- Divide the mince into ping-pong sized balls.
- Add these to the pot and simmer until the soup reaches a dense but desirable consistency. Use more stock if required.
- Garnish with caramelised onions and serve hot.

IN A NUTSHELL

Hearty and delicious, this recipe is sourced from my personal collection. The highlight of this one pot wonder dish is the Baharat masala made at home. This pulao is capable of lulling you into a well-deserved siesta making it ideal for lazy weekends.

METHOD FOR THE BAHARAT

- Dry roast all the ingredients in the Baharat masala list apart from paprika and nutmeg powder for 3-4 minutes. Toss the spices to ensure they don't burn.
- Remove from heat, allow them to cool.
- Grind into a fine powder with paprika and nutmeg powders.
- Keep 1 tbsp aside for later use and keep the rest sealed tightly in a jar.

Gulf Pulao

 90 minutes Serves  8

INGREDIENTS

- 2 tbsps vegetable oil
- 1 kg chicken, a combination of thighs, legs, and breasts.
- 3 tbsps unsalted butter or ghee (clarified butter)
- 2 large onions, diced
- 1 tbsp fresh ginger, minced
- 5 large cloves of garlic, thinly sliced
- 1 hot green chilli, seeded and diced
- 1 tbsp baharat (see recipe below)
- 1 tsp turmeric powder
- 2 large roma tomatoes, diced (or 1 [14 oz] can diced tomatoes, juices drained)
- 2-3 dried limes or loomi, several holes punched throughout each one
- 5 pods of green cardamom
- 1 cinnamon stick 2 inch-long
- ⅛ tsp ground cloves
- 2½ tsps salt
- 2½ cups chicken stock
- 3 tbsps fresh cilantro, chopped
- 2 tbsps fresh parsley, chopped
- 2 cups Tilda Basmati Rice (soaked for at least 15 minutes, then rinsed and drained)
- 1-2 tbsps rosewater

FOR BAHARAT:

- 1 tbsp paprika powder
- ¼ tsp nutmeg powder
- 1 tbsp cumin seeds
- 2 tsps coriander seeds
- ¼ tsp whole green cardamon
- 1 tbsp peppercorns
- 1 cinnamon stick 2 inch-long
- 1 tsp cloves whole

METHOD

- Heat the oil in a large pot over medium high heat and fry the chicken pieces on both sides until the skin is brown and crispy.
- Transfer the chicken to a plate. Leave the remaining oil pot.
- Reduce the heat to medium and add ghee or butter.
- Add onions and sauté until they start turning brown.
- Add ginger, garlic and green chilli pepper. Sauté for another 2 minutes.
- Add the baharat and turmeric and cook for another minute.
- Return the chicken pieces to the pot along with the tomatoes, dried limes, cardamom pods, cinnamon, ground cloves and salt.
- Add the chicken stock and stir to combine. Bring it to a boil, reduce the heat to low, cover and simmer for one hour.
- Add the cilantro, parsley and drained rice and stir to combine. Return it to a boil, reduce the heat to low, cover, and simmer for another 15-20 minutes until the rice is done and has absorbed the liquid.
- Transfer the chicken and rice to a serving dish (either leave the chicken pieces tossed in with the rice, or place the chicken on top of the rice), and sprinkle 1-2 tbsps of rosewater (optional).
- Serve with a green salad and raita.

Bhatkali Sausage Parcel

60-70 minutes | Serves 6-8

IN A NUTSHELL

Bhatkali cuisine is indigenous to Bhatkal in the coastal state of Karnataka. Usually eaten as a snack, these steamed sausage parcels are one of the few well-known dishes from this cuisine. The Bhatkali Sausage Parcel can easily double up as a meal on the go!

INGREDIENTS

¼ kg chicken (or beef) sausages, chopped

1 ⅓ cups of rice

1 coconut, grated

15 green chillies, slit and deseeded

½ cup red chilli paste

1 tbsp turmeric powder

1 tsp red chilli powder

¼ cup ginger-garlic paste

8 onions, finely chopped

Banana leaves/banana leaves to steam

1 tbsp cooking oil

Water as needed

METHOD

- Soak rice in water for at least 4 hours.
- Grind coconut into a fine paste.
- Grind the rice into a thick paste and use water to adjust the consistency. Keep aside.
- Grind the coconut, green chillies, chilli paste, turmeric, red chilli powder, ginger-garlic paste, and onions into a coarse, thick paste.
- Flatten the banana leaves out with a rolling pin and coat the insides of the leaves with oil.
- Spread the rice paste evenly on the leaf leaving an inch on all sides. Repeat this step using the spice paste.
- Place the chopped sausages inside and tie into parcels.
- Steam this mix for about 20 minutes.
- Remove from heat and serve hot.

Written at the Curators of Clay studio

Working with Vicky Ratnani is like getting to hang with one of the coolest cats of the culinary world. We're convinced that if he hadn't become a chef, this man would have been a true blue rock star.

Right from the first time he messaged us – literally out of the blue – saying he'd seen our work, loved it and wanted to see what we could do for him, with every commission, we've worked together like clockwork.

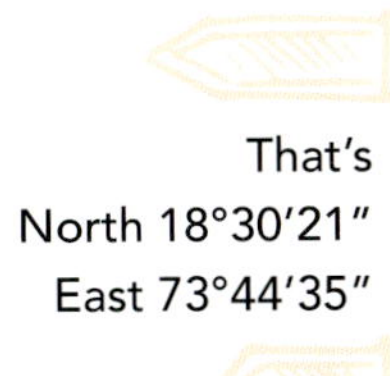

That's
North 18°30′21″
East 73°44′35″

And for this particular project we knew we wanted to pull out all the stops.

After all, it isn't everyday that a celebrated chef gives you a creative brief and then not only grants you creative freedom but also lets you run wild with it!

As a studio, we're very clear that no matter how crazy we get, we focus on functionality and stick to our core belief that our work is art for everyday use.

Over the years, we've experienced first-hand Chef Vicky's inherent ability to cook up a storm with the simplest of ingredients. That's why we were stoked to work on this project with him – a man who truly enjoys his work. This is something we admire immensely and emulate ourselves. We too love what we do for a living.

Every single piece of ceramic that we've crafted for this book has been true to the tenets of our philosophy as full-time potters:

1) Handmade, from start to finish, by one of us.

2) Form follows function.

3) All our work is made to be used, enjoyed and cherished.

At Curators of Clay, we make our own clay, conjure up our own glazes and fire our work personally, in gas-fuelled kilns that are built to our

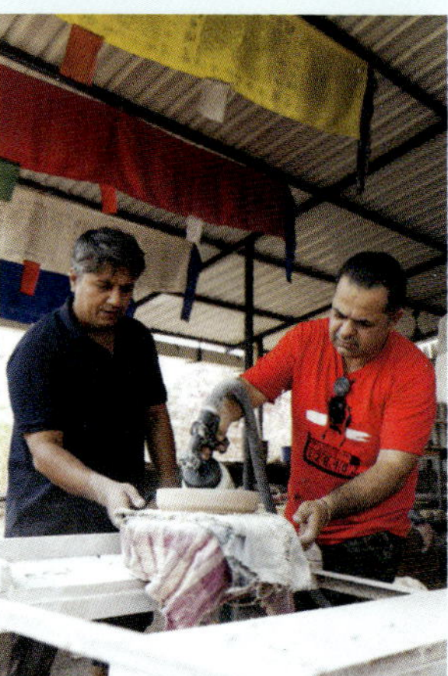

designs. Our aesthetic is entirely contemporary but our approach to it is decidedly old school and we follow time-honoured processes and techniques to craft beautiful functional ceramics.

Just as Chef Vicky himself is a hands-on cook, both Bhairavi and I are potters first. We are craftspersons. Everything else follows.

Crafting high-fired ceramics by hand is an art and a science. If we had to describe the collection we made for this book in one word, it would be 'instinctive'.

The forms, the glazes, the accents and the nuances all came from a gut feeling. For instance, the long platters we made, weren't crafted by rolling out slabs, they were cylinders thrown on the wheel and then cut open to 'unroll' into platters. This created a natural curve and raised the edge so the food wouldn't spill out. For the serving bowls, the lugs were left a little un-glazed on the underside, so that the fingers carrying the bowls wouldn't slip. None of these little details may be noticed, but their functionality is sure to be experienced.

For the look and feel too we went with instinct. We are not traditional potters. We are contemporary craftspersons with a passion to let our work reflect today's world. *Urban Desi* is the best way to describe our milieu. That's precisely what we are, and our work is an extension of our personality!

The most fun part of this project was having Chef Vicky spend time with us in the studio, working alongside us, getting his hands dirty. (And his clothes too!)

For all of us here, life is a pursuit of happiness, beauty and peace; clay is our medium and food is Chef Vicky's!

We hope that along with the food you also enjoy the meticulous attention that we as craftspersons, and Chef Vicky as a connoisseur, have given to the tableware.

– Rohit Kulkarni

Acknowledgements

After having cooked abroad in western kitchens, 19 years later when I moved back to India, I started travelling in India. I was keen on learning about the country through its food, ingredients and of course people. This book features some of my favourite dishes and I would like to thank:

My parents, Prabha Ratnani and Murli Ratnani. I would like to dedicate this book to them.

My lovely wife Piya Ratnani, my daughter Tanisha who is a fabulous cook, my sister- in-law Jyoti , my aunts – Nimma, Deepti, Meena, Reena, Mala – for all their inputs, and feedback.

Tanvi Juwale who helped me research on this book. When I first expressed the idea about this book to her, I explained to her that I want to pen down dishes which are easy, fun to cook and the ingredients should be easily available at any Asian grocery store, anywhere in the world. Her thorough research gave this book an edge.

My friends at Curators of Clay who helped me with customised earthy crockery.

My favourite photographers who have also worked with me in the past on various restaurant and television projects: Aashish who travelled with me, Vinayak who captured the stunning visuals and Piyush who came along with me to the docks where we shot some real cool stuff...I love you guys.

My chefs: Vikram Bhandari, Tuhin, Akshay Bhagat who orchestrated all the preps and made it possible for me to cook and style (yes, I was the cook and stylist on this book).

Lastly, to the Universe.

Glossary

Achar	A pickle native to Indian subcontinent made using spices and oil
Akhrot	Walnut
Amaranth	An ancient pseudo cereal cultivated and consumed by the Aztecs and ancient Indians, also known as Rajgira (Marathi), Chulai (Hindi)
Amchoor	Raw mango powder
Anchovy	Small silver fish usually used for flavouring owing to its distinct salty taste
Appam	A fermented rice batter pancake originating from south India
Artisanal	Hand crafted or hand made food products in small quantities by skilled craftsmen
Arbi/Arvi/Suran	Colocasia
Badam/Badaam	Almonds
Besan	Gram flour
Bhakri	A thick flatbread made with cereals and grains
Biryani	A slow cooked rice dish made with an assortment of spices and meat
Bhee	A Sindhi word for lotus root or stem
Bhindi	Okra
Bhuna	A process of sautéing the spices with minimal hot oil
Chaap	Hindi word for ribs. Alternatively, a vegetarian mock meat substitute made using cottage cheese or soy
Chai	A tea concoction made with milk and spices
Chapati	A wheat flatbread usually dry roasted on a griddle
Chawal	Rice
Cheeni	Sugar
Chironji	Cuddapah almonds
Chutney	A dip for appetisers, kebabs, and snacks usually made with herbs
Chikki	A brittle usually made with either with jaggery or jaggery with peanuts, cashews and assortments of dry fruit
Daal	An umbrella term for lentil or lentil curry often eaten with rice
Daab	Bengali word for tender coconut
Dalchini	Cinnamon
Dhansak	A Parsi-Irani meat and lentil curry often relished with rice
Doodh	Milk

Dum	A slow steam or pressure cooking process
Elaichi	Cardamom
Fenugreek seeds	Methi
Fennel	Saunf
Garam Masala	A commonly used spice mix either whole or powdered
Ghee	Clarified butter
Gosht	Meat, mutton or goat meat to be precise
Gur	Jaggery
Haldi	Turmeric
Halwa	An umbrella term for desserts made with ghee, milk solids, nuts, raisins, and sugar
Imli	Tamarind
Jaitoon/ Zaitoon	Olives
Javitri	Mace
Jeera	Cumin
Jhinga/Jheenga	Shrimp
Khoya	Condensed milk solids made by boiling milk over a slow flame f or several hours
Kewda	Screwpine flower, the extract of which is used to enhance the aromatics of dishes such as biryani, pulao, and more
Kabuli Chana	Chickpeas/garbanzo beans
Kadhi	A yoghurt based gravy made with besan
Kaju	Cashews
Kali Mirch	Black pepper
Kalonji	Nigella seed also, black onion seeds
Karipatta	Curry leaves
Kasoori Methi	Sun dried fenugreek leaves
Kathal	Jackfruit
Kebab	An array of bite-sized seasoned meat or vegetable dishes usually served as appetisers, sides, or snacks
Keema	Minced meat also known as qeema
Kesar /Zaffran	Saffron
Khopra/Nariyal	Coconut
Khus-Khus	Poppy seeds
Kishmish	Golden raisins also known as sultanas

Kofta	A general term for mealtball but also a mock meatball in vegetarian recipes
Kotu	Buckwheat
Kulfi	Indian frozen dessert that resembles a popsicle made with milk and milk solids
Luchi	See Puri
Lal Mirch	Red chili
Laung	Cloves
Lasan/Lehsun	Garlic
Lassi	A yogurt-based drink that can be made either sweet or savory
Lauki	Bottle gourd
Machi	Fish
Maida	All purpose flour
Malai	Cream mostly a creamy-lactose based or derived cream
Makai	Hindi for corn
Masala	A mixture of spices used in Indian cooking
Masoor Dal	Red lentils
Matar	Green peas
Meetha	Sweet or could mean dessert
Methi	Fenugreek
Mirch	Chili and/or spice
Mithai	Sweet or dessert
Moong Dal	A small yellow lentil
Murgh	Chicken
Naan	A flatbread cooked in a tandoor
Namak	Salt
Nariyal	Coconut
Nimboo	Lime
Pao	An inheritance of the Portugese, pao is a type of bread natively eaten in the parts of Indian that was colonised by them
Papad/ Pappadam	Thin crispy lentil or cereal wafer
Parotta	A flaky flatbread made using cereal which is commonly eaten in t he Malabar region
Paratha	A stuffed flatbread
Pulao	Similar to the middle-eastern pilaf, pulao is a rice dish usually made with vegetables and/or meat

Puri	A deep fried flatbread also called luchi in Bengali cuisine
Pakora	An umbrella term for deep fried fritters made using an array of vegetables and/or meat
Palak	Spinach
Panch Phoron	A spice blend commonly used in Bengali
Paneer	Indian cottage cheese usually consumed as a vegetarian protein
Phool Makhana	Fox nuts
Qeema	See keema
Qubani	Apricots
Rai	Mustard seeds
Raita	A curd based dip often served with biryani
Rohu	A freshwater fish found in India
Roti	Read chapati
Saag	A vegetable dish made with leafy greens, a staple for most Indian households
Sabudana	Tapioca pearls
Sambar	A spicy south Indian lentil soup with vegetables
Samosa	A deep fried Indian snack made by stuffing spiced potato or mince
Sarson	Mustard greens or seeds
Saunf	Fennel seeds
Seb or Saib	Apple
Sooji/Suji	Semolina
Toor Dal	Split pigeon peas
Tadka	The process of tempering also known as bagar or chhaunk
Tandoor	A clay oven
Tandoori	A dish cooked in a tandoor
Tej Patta	Indian bay leaf
Tel	Oil
Tikka	Grilled meat or vegetables pieces marinated in a spice mix.
Tikki	Moderate or bite-sized cutlets usually made with potatoes or meat or both
Til	Sesame seeds
Urad dal	Black gram
Yakhni	A yogurt based meat curry or stew originating from Kashmir

Index

L

M

N

P

Q

R

S

T

Z

coffee